heal
your
soul

heal *your* soul

10 ways to find inner peace and unlock your potential

Sue Minns

CICO BOOKS
LONDON NEW YORK

This edition published in 2023 by CICO Books
An imprint of Ryland Peters & Small Ltd
20–21 Jockey's Fields, London, WC1R 4BW
341 E 116th St, New York, NY 10029

www.rylandpeters.com

10 9 8 7 6 5 4 3 2 1

First published in 2002 as *Be Your Own
Soul Doctor*

A CIP catalog record for this book
is available from the Library of Congress
and the British Library.

ISBN: 978 1 80065 232 3

Printed in China

Designer: Louise Turpin
Illustrations: Jacqui Mair and Sam Wilson
Photo on page 41: vetre—stock.adobe.com
Photo on page 64: courtesy of Corbis Stockmarket

Art director: Sally Powell
Creative director: Leslie Harrington
Head of production: Patricia Harrington
Publishing manager: Penny Craig

Contents

Introduction   6

CHAPTER 1
The Body–Mind Link   8
Your body as a car   10
A new you in seven years   11
Our communicating hemispheres   12
Body language   13
How does body language work?   17
Every body part tells a story   21
Past memories   22
Body-mind journey   24

CHAPTER 2
The Power of Breath   28
Breathing and meditation   30
How your body breathes   30
The mind connection   32
Breathing and your soul   32
Breathing and meditation   36
Meditation techniques   40

CHAPTER 3
The Aura and the Universal Energy Field   44
Sense beyond reason   46
The rhythm of life   47
What is an aura?   48
The etheric body   52
The astral or emotional body   54
The mental or causal body   55
The soul or causal body   57
Auric egg visualization   58

CHAPTER 4

The Body Chakras 62

Chakra origins 64
Having enough of everything 67
Creativity and the sacral chakra 70
The solar plexus and identity 73
The heart under siege 78
Journey through the chakras 86
Crystal power 90

CHAPTER 5

Healing 92

The caduceus 94
Balancing our life force 94
Tuning in 95
Who can be a healer? 96
The healing ritual 97
Painful areas 98
Absent or distant healing 99
Color healing 99
Sound healing 100
Simple healing techniques 101
Healing tune-up 102

CHAPTER 6

The Psychic Internet 104

Logging on 107
Psychic abilities 107
Opening up to new energies 108
Accessing the psychic highway 110
Feeling psychic energy 111
Emotional sensitivity to feelings 112
Thinking—listening with the mind 113
Special messages 114
The wrong messages 114
Intuition, visual imagery, and inner knowing 116
Inner seeing exercise 116
The help of spirit guides 119
How to stay protected 120
Through the psychic gateway 124

CHAPTER 7

The Inner Child and Soul 126

Karmic influences 128
Soul contracts 129
The inner soul child 130
Finding your inner child 135
Journey to the sanctuary to meet
    my inner child 136

CHAPTER 8

Karma and and Reincarnation 138

The mysteries of life and rebirth 140
Marks from past lives 141
Past-life therapy 143
Why consult a past-life therapist? 143
The law of karma 145
Memories of the past 146
Young or old souls? 146
Why do people get chronically ill? 147
What about soul mates? 148
Journey into my archives 150

Helpful Practices 153

Looking inside 154
Healthy mind, body, and soul 157

Further Reading 159
Index 160

Introduction

Our deepest fear is not that we are inadequate. Our deepest fear is that we are powerful beyond measure. It is our light, not our darkness, that most frightens us. We ask ourselves "Who am I to be brilliant, gorgeous, talented, fabulous?". Actually, who are you not to be? You are a child of God. Your playing small doesn't serve the world. There's nothing enlightened about shrinking so that other people won't feel insecure around you. We are all meant to shine, as children do … and as we let our light shine, we unconsciously give other people permission to do the same. As we're liberated from our own fear, our presence automatically liberates others.

From President Nelson Mandela's Inauguration Speech, 1994

We are living in extraordinary times—probably the most extraordinary times in our history as we know it. We are in the process of making a quantum leap in consciousness, and the tools we have used in the past to make sense of the world in which we live are no longer serving us. We find ourselves searching for meaning in our lives—meaning that, for many, is not provided by structured religion. Who are we, for heaven's sake? And what on earth are we doing here? How do we bring body, mind, and soul into meaningful balance?

Finding out who we are

We do not have to go to the other side of the globe, or sit for years just thinking, to discover who we are. The answers to everything we need to know are within each of us. We are not bodies, minds, and emotions that have a vague sense of soul (whatever that is) somewhere in the background. We are souls, inhabiting these bodies of ours and we can use our minds and emotions to support the purpose of the soul once we acknowledge its presence. Our bodies feel things, our minds think about things—our soul simply "knows." As well as always being present within us, our souls also exist outside our human understanding of time and space. They remember where "Home" is, and carry the memory, or imprint, of all our previous life incarnations and experiences. The soul knows what situations are required on the Earth plane for development and learning.

This book is about learning as re-membering who you really are. It is about discovering that you are more than you thought you were, and the most important tool for this discovery is an open mind and an understanding that spirit and matter, body and soul are not to be kept in separate camps. For this part of our journey, they are traveling together. A soul without a body could not possibly experience all there is to understand about life on Earth, and a body without a soul would take life down to the basic, instinctual level of survival.

This book aims to put you in touch with your experience of communicating with your soul, combining information with practical exercises so that you get a sense of what this means.

How to use this book

You will benefit most if you work through this book slowly. You might take each chapter as a focus for a week, then each week to practice the meditations, go through the exercises and contemplate on the meaning they have for you.

Buy a special journal for your notes. This will help you crystallize the information coming from your psyche or unconscious mind, which is directly linked to your soul. In this journal you can also record your dreams (more information from your unconscious), your experiences as you do the medit tions, and for noting any changes in awareness.

THE SOUL FOCUS BOX: You can use this as a focus to take you into meditation, or as a daily affirmation, something you say to yourself before you join the busy routine of everyday life. It will act as a compass, helping to keep you on course as you move through the day.

THE MEDITATIONS AND VISUALIZATIONS: Record these so that you can play them back to yourself. By listening back to them, your body will more easily relax and follow the stream of words. When you are recording, speak clearly and slowly. Pause at the end of paragraphs,

and where you need to. Recording in the first person also helps the left, analytical brain to cooperate. Make certain you are fully back in your body at the end of a meditation by taking deep breaths, and gently stretching your body.

REMINDERS: You will find these at the end of each chapter. They offer a summary of key points and suggestions for new ways of being, which can be incorporated into your daily life. But take it slowly. If you try to change too much too fast, or practice too many new things all at once, you could easily feel overwhelmed and give up. Just take this wonderful journey one step at a time. A recommendation to read the end of a book is not usually made in the introduction, but in this instance you may find it useful to refer to Chapter 9, Helpful Practices, which gives guidance on ways to introduce and support spiritual practice into your life.

It is also important to remember that nothing changes in isolation. You may find that as you explore and change the way you see things, people around you may feel uncomfortable. It may mean that some of your friends and acquaintances will change. Perhaps, if they are resistant to change themselves, they will try to condemn your new experiences. Do not worry, this is all part of the new journey that you are taking. Opening yourself up to new ideas and perspectives means that you become more in tune with yourself. We're not talking about you attaining instant enlightenment, but going on a narrow path that begins to widen into a road with an infinitely more interesting view.

CHAPTER 1

The Body-Mind Link

As is the human body, so is the cosmic body
As is the human mind, so is the cosmic mind
As is the microcosm, so is the macrocosm
As is the atom, so is the Universe.
The Upanishads

What is the "body-mind" link?

This is how the body speaks its mind through actions, illness and pleasure. This link is like an everyday news update on your progress in life. Like dreams, your body reveals unconscious or conscious problems and desires.

How can it benefit me?

This is how the body speaks its mind through actions, illness and pleasure. This link is like an everyday news update on your progress in life. Like dreams, your body reveals unconscious or conscious problems and desires.

How do I start?

Look in the mirror. Observe your posture, shape, and the parts of you that you love and hate.

If we think about our bodies at all, we may feel that they are
just physical vehicles that keep us glued to the face of the earth,
full of appetites and desires that continually need resisting or fulfilling.
Some of us may be conditioned to believe that we should deny
our fleshy container, keep our eyes focused on heaven, and identify
the boy as the source of pain and suffering rather than joy and delight.

Yet the body is our greatest ally on the path of spiritual growth,
because it lives in the moment, in the "now." It gives you valuable
feedback on if you are acting according to your soul purpose.
It informs you on your negative, destructive thoughts, and
shows you where you are storing unexpressed feelings. It is
your vehicle for crossing from the level of physical reality
to the expanded, conscious awareness of who you really are.

This earthly body of ours contains a space-time travel vehicle, a magic child, a barometer, a compass, a pharmacy complete with pharmacist, and a library full of archives.

Your body as a car

Stop for a moment, and imagine that if your body was a car, what might it look like? Write it down, or draw it, in a journal. Then write, or draw it, as you would like it to be.

What do you know about your car? Do you just jump in and hope it will get you from A to B as quickly as possible, or do you know and understand what goes on under the bonnet? Obviously, it needs gas, or you won't be going anywhere. What kind of fuel do you fill yourself up with? Do you pay attention to the little knocks and rattles, or hope that they will sort themselves out? Many people ignore the rising needle on the temperature gauge until steam gushes out of the bonnet and the car comes to a grinding halt. Maintenance work is only carried out because of a looming service. However, the attitude and awareness of you, the driver, is essential for the smooth running and overall performance of your body, or car. Of course, this earthly body of yours is infinitely more than just a car—it contains a space-time travel vehicle, a magic child, a barometer, a compass, a pharmacy complete with pharmacist, and a library full of archives. It is a universe and also an atom within that universe; it is a miracle, and without it, we would not feel a thing.

A new you in seven years

Let us take a closer look at this miracle that we take so much for granted. Perhaps the most important point to understand is that the body has its own consciousness—it has a mind of its own, it hears every word you say, or rather feels, every thought you think—and translates those thoughts into reality. It metabolizes your thoughts in the same way that it metabolizes a tomato sandwich. There are over 50 trillion cells in your body and each one has over 3 million different ways of communicating; another information superhighway. Life and death at the cellular level are the same as night and day to us. Each cell is replicated by a new cell stored with the identical information of the deceased, so a scar continues to be a scar, even though the wound was experienced long ago.

Our bodies have an inner pharmacy and pharmacist that goes about his business without our conscious knowledge. Hair just keeps on growing, baked potatoes get digested, and every cell gets replaced when it has reached its sell-by date. The "you" that is reading this will be totally different from top to bottom, head to toe, skin to bone-cells, in the space of seven years. There will not be one cell that is the same as it is at this moment.

Medical science is finally beginning to acknowledge the interconnection between what happens in our bodies, and what goes on in our heads. As technology advances, illness created by the interaction between our minds and bodies will become a provable fact, rather than being labeled as psychosomatic. It will become possible to detect the tumor in the auric field before it becomes a physical reality. This new science has the elaborate title of psycho-neuroimmunology, or PNI.

Soul work is about understanding who you are and expressing your true self. When this happens, there is balance between what you feel inside and how you live externally.

Our communicating hemispheres

To understand what our bodies try to tell us, it is first important to know that although we might assume that we think with a single mind, this is not the case. We have twin "travelers" living beside one another in our cranium— the left and right hemispheres of our brain— and they each have very different functions, and very different ways of experiencing, translating, and storing information about the world. Usually, one of the two hemispheres is dominant, and in our current society we have been encouraged to use and trust the processes of our left brain. But our left and right brains need to get together and work in harmony, so that life is experienced from a point of balance.

Imagine that you are about to do a jigsaw. The right brain holds the picture on the lid

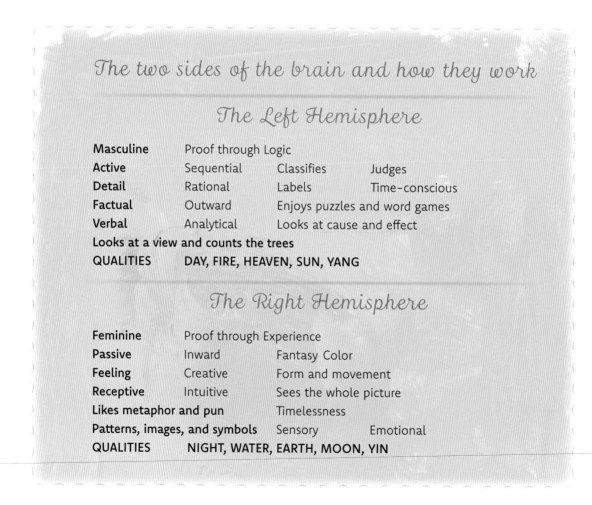

The two sides of the brain and how they work

The Left Hemisphere

Masculine	Proof through Logic		
Active	Sequential	Classifies	Judges
Detail	Rational	Labels	Time-conscious
Factual	Outward	Enjoys puzzles and word games	
Verbal	Analytical	Looks at cause and effect	
Looks at a view and counts the trees			
QUALITIES	DAY, FIRE, HEAVEN, SUN, YANG		

The Right Hemisphere

Feminine	Proof through Experience		
Passive	Inward	Fantasy Color	
Feeling	Creative	Form and movement	
Receptive	Intuitive	Sees the whole picture	
Likes metaphor and pun		Timelessness	
Patterns, images, and symbols	Sensory	Emotional	
QUALITIES	NIGHT, WATER, EARTH, MOON, YIN		

of the box, while the left brain sorts the pieces out and works out what bits go where. Obviously you need both of these two sides of the brain working together in order to complete the puzzle.

Unfortunately, we do not usually allow these partners to collaborate on making sense of the puzzle that is life, and we value the functions of one side more than the other. Perhaps we have become overly concerned with sorting out which bit goes where without holding the overall vision of our life. Or, we may live in the clouds and be totally out of touch with the practicalities that have to be dealt with. We are so involved with the dream that we forget that bills have to be paid and the doors have to be locked. Listing the different functions of the left and right brain may give you an idea of which side of your brain you use predominantly.

Both of these twin travelers think and reason, but they do operate in very different ways, and it is obvious which one of these we are educated and encouraged to use predominantly. But we need the attributes of both of them to live in balance in this physical, material world.

Body language

To understand anyone, we need to be able to communicate. Body language is a term often used these days, but what does it mean? How do our bodies speak to us? Do we need a dictionary or glossary of terms? No, but you do need to recognize that the body works closely with the unconscious mind, and the language of the unconscious mind is image and metaphor. You will probably not be able

One of the ways in which the body speaks its mind is through posture. When a person is depressed, the body becomes lethargic.

to access the body's messages and information through verbal language—it uses a different tongue. The right hemisphere of your brain, your right mind, will be your translator.

One of the ways in which the body speaks its mind is through posture. When a person is depressed, the body becomes lethargic, wanting to slump and hide. On the other hand, it is easy to identify people who feel on top of the world. Their whole body looks as though it feels good to be alive—life is an exciting challenge, an adventure, a discovery. When the body feels that it needs to protect itself, it will automatically cross its arms (protecting the Solar Plexus chakra, the center of personal power—see page 63) and cross the legs to defend itself against perceived "invasive"

*Jumping for joy, a leap of faith,
or dancing with delight show
our innate connection with
our instinctive, inner selves.*

energies. Avoiding eye contact is another way that the body maintains defence: to look someone in the eye may mean that they will see who you are, and that might be frightening. Lie detectors register body signals to discover whether the mind is telling the truth. The body never lies.

The most obvious way that the body speaks to us is by expressing its disease, its discomfort about the way that we are living our lives, about thought patterns and emotions that are not in line with our spiritual growth and development. We have become accustomed to rushing to the doctor to fix the symptom, but this is effectively gagging an important messenger. When the car blows up, we take it to the garage to get it fixed quickly, so that

we can continue to hurtle from here to there. Perhaps it would be more useful to stop and wonder why your car continually overheats in certain situations. By taking the approach that disease is a message from our body that is simply trying to communicate an imbalance that needs to be addressed, we will eventually uncover the cause behind the symptom instead of sticking a plaster over the wound and hoping it will get better and go away. Swedenborg, the Dutch visionary and scientist, said, "Every natural physical manifestation has a relationship to a corresponding non-physical state of being." In other words, the visible and invisible, the conscious and unconscious, spirit and matter, are all inextricably linked. Science, has followed a different train of thought, subscribing to the Cartesian view that mind and body are separate, and that the universe and everything in it is a machine that gradually runs down from Big Bang to Big Crunch.

Every part of our bodies gives us specific information about ourselves, because it has received repeated messages, both conscious and unconscious, that it translates into physical reality in order that we may pay attention to

Emotions are written on the body. Facial expression and minor physical ailments tell other people, and ourselves, how we are feeling.

What we tell our bodies

I feel heartbroken about his death

⋄⋄⋄⋄⋄⋄⋄⋄⋄⋄⋄⋄

I'm going out of my mind with worry/grief/fear

⋄⋄⋄⋄⋄⋄⋄⋄⋄⋄⋄⋄

I am dead on my feet

⋄⋄⋄⋄⋄⋄⋄⋄⋄⋄⋄⋄

Something is eating away at me

⋄⋄⋄⋄⋄⋄⋄⋄⋄⋄⋄⋄

I'll give him the cold shoulder

⋄⋄⋄⋄⋄⋄⋄⋄⋄⋄⋄⋄

I won't bite off more that I can chew

⋄⋄⋄⋄⋄⋄⋄⋄⋄⋄⋄⋄

She's a pain in the neck

⋄⋄⋄⋄⋄⋄⋄⋄⋄⋄⋄⋄

I can't see my way out of this

⋄⋄⋄⋄⋄⋄⋄⋄⋄⋄⋄⋄

I'm losing my grip

⋄⋄⋄⋄⋄⋄⋄⋄⋄⋄⋄⋄

I don't want to hear what you are saying

areas of imbalance. The language of body is metaphor, remember, so hands, for example, speak not about holding kettles or gripping pens, but more about being in touch with life. Here are some more examples: the heart may tell us whether we beat in time to the rhythm of life; our digestive system gives us clues about whether we retain unwanted matter or shoot things through without assimilating. Our feet and legs may tell us how we feel about stepping out in life, and if we have our feet on the ground.

The body continually strives to be in a state of homeostasis, or balance. The balance of an anorexic continually hears: "It's not safe to get bigger." The gut of someone worried and frustrated hears: "I'm sick and tired of this," and produces an ulcer to prove the point. The eyes of someone stuck or confused may get the message: "I can't see things clearly," and need ever-stronger spectacles. Imagine what your body might do to alert you to imbalance if it were continually hearing the messages listed on the left.

These may be conscious or unconscious thoughts or statements about things going on in your life—it doesn't make any difference. If there is any energy-charge to each thought or feeling it will register on the subtle anatomy, on those "bodies" of yours that are non-physical, and which make up your auric field (see p. 74).

Repetition of the same feeling piles static onto static until it becomes an aggregation, or complex, of energy held in the aura or chakra system. This prevents a free flow of energy in that area, and will begin to take effect at a cellular level in the form of imbalance or disease.

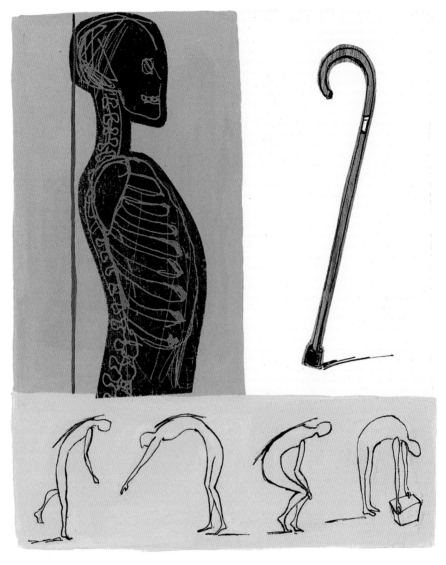

Back pain is a common and debilitating ailment, as the spine is the core of our bodies and central to our wellbeing. In soul terms, back problems can be associated with feeling overburdened by life.

How does body language work?

To understand the body's language, we need to know a bit about its make-up. There are three primary ways in which cells are formed: hard tissue, soft tissue and fluids. How do these messengers speak about their state of health?

BACK PAIN Hard tissue cells make up our bones. Our bones are our core structure. Our spinal column is the central axis of our being; it supports the rest of us. Millions of people suffer from back pain these days (what is the body saying about feeling unsupported?) Certainly, many people lead sedentary lives that do not encourage a healthy posture, but perhaps there

Often, we subconsciously build fat to protect us from painful memories; at a soul level, this can be a reason for obesity. 'Life can be sweeter when there is less need to cover ourselves up.

is something more behind that chronic, lower-back pain. Consider what split, at our core level, is being manifested by the body to get our attention.

WEIGHT PROBLEMS: Soft tissue is flesh, fat, muscle, nerves, skin, and organs. The soft tissue of our bodies reflects our mental energy, our hidden mental patterns, attitudes, behavior, and experiences. We build fat to protect us from painful memories. Many women seem to have a disposition to accumulate weight round their hips and thighs. Is this the body making a literal statement about the need to protect her vulnerable sexuality? Obesity is on the increase in Western society. Is this because the body has translated the message from the unconscious that there is a lack, there is a deep need for inner nourishment, that has been ignored? Or perhaps the body has got the message that it is not really safe to be here, so has to add weight to itself in an attempt to tell the conscious mind that it does indeed exist.

MUSCLE TENSION AND STIFFNESS: What about tension and stiffness in the muscles? Those shoulders that feel as though they are made of concrete may be saying that it is difficult to shoulder life's burdens. The mental stress that we put ourselves under gives the body the message that it is necessary to be on continual red alert, ready to fight (for example, bracing the upper torso) or to flee—by tightening the buttocks, abdomen, and thighs. If this state of tension is maintained throughout the day, the muscles never get a chance to relax and release the toxic by-products of being on red alert, because the tension is not turned into action and the adrenaline just keeps on pumping.

POOR SKIN: Our skin is the largest organ of the body and the interface between our inner and outer worlds. An angry skin condition could be the result of a different irritation; is there a situation that makes you feel as though you want to erupt? If these thoughts or feelings are repressed, your skin will expose them for you.

Being in a tight spot can be quite literal—"angry"—looking spots can reflect suppressed emotions that simply surface via the skin.

Fluids are linked to our emotions. Ailments that hinder the flow of fluids and blood in the body, such as circulatory problems, can be related to emotional blocks.

energy. Blood can freeze with fear or boil with anger. It is our liquid life force. Hardening of the arteries can indicate a resistance to and hardening of our emotional energies. Clots in the cardiovascular system may mean we are blocking the flow of life through us in some way.

SWOLLEN GLANDS, COLDS: Lymph is the garbage-collector of the body and swollen glands may be the body's way of saying: "I getting congested with toxic thoughts in here — please pay attention". A course of antibiotics will almost certainly sort it out, but we need to pay attention to the fact that our immune system has become over-worked and depleted, that too much energy is being spent on defence in there. Think of the last time you had a cold or sinus problems. What might your body have been trying to tell you?

URINARY INFECTIONS: The kidneys and bladder are part of the waste disposal team. Water represents emotions, therefore urinary infections, such as cystitis and prostatitis, are thought to occur when there are unexpressed or painful thoughts and feelings concerning relationships and sexuality.

EMOTIONAL BLOCKS: Fluids represent our emotions. Like the planet we live on, over 75 per cent of the human body is liquid: water, blood, urine, lymph, sweat, saliva, tears, endocrine, and sexual secretions. We came into physical being in the waters within our mother's wombs. Fluids bathe our entire being and are like a great ocean moving within us, like tides flowing with our desires, feelings, and impulses. These fluids create excitement, warmth, and

Our feelings should anchor us, but sometimes repressed emotions, or too many problems, can weigh us down.

Growth and restriction are important issues in soul work. Ask yourself if your environment or your attitudes are at the root of your current feelings—do you feel free to express your personality, or sit tight?

Every body part tells a story

All parts of your body will give you clues, in metaphoric language, that will direct you to bringing about balance in your life. The respiratory system indicates your ability to breathe in life. The cardiovascular system speaks about the flow of life. The lymphatic system is the messenger of waste and toxic thought forms, and the gastrointestinal system will tell you about your ability to digest the life process. Your eyes might have something to say about how you really see life. Your back will tell you about what you might be trying to put behind you and whether you feel supported.

Each hemisphere of the brain is connected with a side of the body and there is a neural crossover behind the eyes, which means the left brain is concerned with the right side of the body, and vice versa. So, discomfort expressed on the right-hand side of the body may be connected to the masculine, yang aspect of your nature—the positive, out-going, active side of you that is governed by the left brain. Anything amiss on the left-hand side of the body, conversely, may be connected to the feminine, yin receiving aspect of your Self (the right brain).

Stop and think about the times when you or others were being spoken to by your Body and see if you can make the connection between the ailment—a symptom—and the deeper cause that lies behind it.

Our bodies also have the most phenomenal memory ability. Stored in the body-memory archives is everything from the colour of the shoes you wore at your third birthday party, to every car registration number in the supermarket car park you were in yesterday. It remembers how to ride a bike, drive a car and eat spaghetti, so that you do not have to re-learn these skills the next time you use them. It may also store the memories from previous lifetimes by producing birthmarks where there were wounds before, or physical disabilities that echo past traumas to the body.

The memory of our first pair of school shoes, to how to ride a bicycle to the art of eating spaghetti (above and left), are stored in the brain on a unique, internal CD.

Past memories

There is the documented story of a woman who had a heart transplant. After receiving her new heart, she developed a quite uncharacteristic liking for a certain type of beer and an overwhelming desire to eat chicken McNuggets. She was also visited each night in her dreams by a young man who kept on appearing and saying that she was the new owner of his heart. Deciding that the mystery needed to be unravelled, she came upon the perhaps not-so-astonishing discovery that the young man in her dreams looked identical to her heart donor, and that he had been run over and killed on his way home from the local MacDonalds. He had just had his usual chicken McNuggets, washed down by his favourite beer.

Rather like the trunk of a tree, our body stores the memory of what happens to us year by year, moment by moment. If you cut through the trunk of a tree, you will find it has rings that indicate its annual growth. You can also tell from the rings if the year was a good one for the tree, with ample rain and sun to encourage its growth, or whether conditions were hard and difficult. As with a tree, our early years of growth are instrumental in forming the nature of who we become in later life. What happened to us as children is registered, from ice-cream treats to withering glances, and our body will create the physical response it experienced then, if the same messages keep on being fed to it.

Think back to your first years. Did you find yourself "bonsai'd," or planted in a pot that was too constricting? Were you over-watered? Perhaps, on the other hand, the hold was too loose, giving you feelings of insecurity?

You may have found yourself as an apple tree, growing in an olive grove, striving all the time to be an olive tree like the others and denying your essential apple-ness. Because we needed to survive in what must often have been experienced by our inner, Divine Child as a gross, dense, and unfriendly world, we set up these patterns of behaviour in order to get love. Of course we needed food, air and water to survive, but love is the fundamental requirement for healthy growth and development. Without it, the inner child withers and splits off. The body remembers all that went on back then, and will continue to use the same strategies for coping in a frightening, often loveless world. When someone speaks to you or looks at you in a certain way, do you find yourself reacting in a way that seems irrational?

Are you continually searching in another person for the love your mother never gave you? Whatever your age now, the inner child (see pages 120–132) still wants its needs met. No matter how self-reliant you are as a woman, there is a little girl in there who is vulnerable and needs help, and no matter how macho the man, there is a little boy inside craving warmth and affection. Bringing this into conscious awareness allows us to let go of childish reactions that do not serve us as adults. By recognizing our patterns, we can collect our "inner children" who got left behind, and tell them that they no longer have to fear for their survival. There is a loving, aware parent available now—you—who will take care of their needs. It is through our bodies that we can find our inner children and bring them home. Finding her or him and bringing them into your

Soul focus:

My body is the vehicle for my soul's experience on Earth. It is a living, conscious being through which my soul may experience the physical universe.

◇◇◇◇◇◇◇◇◇◇◇◇◇◇◇

Note: Be aware of how and where you hold your feelings. Where might you feel guilt? is there any anger or resentment tucked away in your upper thighs or clenched teeth? What is your blocked nose trying to tell you?

◇◇◇◇◇◇◇◇◇◇◇◇◇◇◇

Notice how you walk and sit.

◇◇◇◇◇◇◇◇◇◇◇◇◇◇◇

When you eat your meals, don't do it standing in the kitchen or watching television —pay attention to the fuel going into your tank, and be mindful as you eat.

current life is a crucial part of the soul's journey. John Bradshaw's pioneering book, *Homecoming*, is highly recommended for further exploration.

We need to remember that we are spiritual beings in human bodies, and not bodies that are sometimes visited by a soul. It is also vital to acknowledge the part our body plays in the soul's journey. In the West we have become obsessed with the power of our minds to accumulate more and more. If we do pay attention to our bodies, it is mostly because we are unhappy with them—we want to change the shape of them in some way, or because they have let us down. Poor body! It spends all its time adjusting to the commands coming from the dictator in the control tower, who never stops to reflect for a moment on the needs and requirements of the faithful workforce.

Stop and remember the last time you did something for the exclusive pleasure of your body (apart from lovemaking). Pamper your senses through massage, bathing, and sleep.

Body-mind journey

Having followed the instructions in the Introduction on how to make your own visualization and meditation tapes (see page 8), prepare for your first inner journey.

Disconnect the phone and make sure you won't be disturbed.

Find a comfortable chair that supports your back, and sit in it with a straight spine (see page 35).

Imagine that there is an invisible string holding your head in place.

Put your hands, palms upward, on your thighs.

Take some deep, easy breaths and begin to relax, remembering that this journey is to help you get in touch with the consciousness of your body.

Allow your body to supply you with the information.
When you are ready, press the play button.

✳ Sitting comfortably, I breathe out tension, starting with my feet and ankles, I breathe out tension... I breathe out tension in my calves and knees, tension leaves my legs, allowing them to relax.

✳ I breathe out tension from my abdomen and buttocks, and my solar plexus... As my body begins to relax, it begins to remember.

✳ I breathe out tension in my chest now, and let the feeling of relaxation move down my arms to my wrists and hands—my fingers feel light... I breathe out tension in my shoulders, they remember how it feels to be free... I breathe out tension in my neck and head, my scalp and all the little muscles in my forehead smooth out as my eyeballs relax, and my jaw relaxes. I feel calm and deeper relaxed.

✳ With my body relaxed, I imagine that I can see a mirror image of myself, it gets smaller and smaller until it is so small it could sit on the head of a pin. Now I imagine this very small me enters my body and finds itself travelling down to arrive on the inside of my left foot. How might I feel inside my left foot? What is the scenery like in here? All the different structures in my left foot—bones, muscles, and tendons that all work together to keep me up and running. I begin to explore myself from the inside, to get in touch with what my body might want to tell me. I start to travel up the inside of my left leg, checking the knee, is it flexible? Going up my thigh, moving into my pelvis and before exploring this, I will just travel down to the bottom of my right leg, into my right foot, moving up through the ankle, the knee and the thigh, noticing if there are any areas that don't feel quite right, or where there might be some pain or stiffness. Now I travel into the pelvic girdle, where a lot of things happen. I let my inner representative look around to see if there is an area that needs calming, clearing or just acknowledging. How does the waste disposal department feel? And all those parts that make up the reproductive team? Now I move into my stomach; how does it feel about what I put into it?

✳ I move in to check my liver, my pancreas, my kidneys. It doesn't matter that I don't know exactly where they are, or what they look like, my inner representative will instinctively find them and get a sense of what they might feel like saying. Now my lungs, do they get fully inspired when I breathe in life?

✳ And now I'll have a look at my heart. Are you beating to my true rhythm? Are you strong and healthy, are you frightened about anything? And how is my heart of hearts? Can you sing about life? Or is there something missing... are you closed or open? If you could speak, heart, what might you like to say? All these vital organs that keep my show on the road, I'd like to thank you for all the silent work you do. Now I'll just travel into my shoulders and release any tension about the burdens you carry. Moving down my arms into my hands and fingers, are you in touch with life, fingers? My little self now travels into my neck and throat—this important place where I give voice to my thoughts and feelings, are there any constrictions here? Do I speak up and speak out? Into my head, the control tower. Now, eyes, are you seeing clearly, or is your vision clouded by the past. Nose, can you smell all that life has to offer, and what about you, mouth? Can you taste the flavor of things? And speak the truth?

✳ Now I've journeyed through my inner space, I'll take a little time to re-visit somewhere that might need specific attention, checking my backbone as I go and asking how it feels about supporting everything in there. I will travel to a place where there might be pain or discomfort, getting a sense of whether this area feels hard or soft, hot or cold. Is this old, or something more recent? What might it say about energy that seems to collect here, instead of moving freely... How can I release this block so that healing can take place? I listen to what my body might have to say. I acknowledge all the work it does, and I take this time to give it my full attention (give yourself some minutes of silence on the tape).

✳ In a moment it will be time for my little inner self to leave, so I'll thank my body for any insights or information it has given me, and for the miraculous team work that's carried out, moment by moment. I will promise to be more aware of how body expresses its discomfort about the thoughts and directions that come from the control tower, and then I will begin to bring my focus back into my everyday reality. Slowly and gently I become aware of the sounds around me. I take some deep breaths, I move my toes and fingers, and when I'm ready, I will open my eyes, feeling lighter and brighter than before.

At this point you might like to get up and go and have a look at yourself in the mirror and just acknowledge your body by saying,

"My soul cannot experience life on this
Earth without you.
Thank you for everything you do".

CHAPTER 2

The Power of Breath

Don't go outside your house to see the answers.
My friend, don't bother with that excursion.
Inside your body there are flowers.
One flower has a thousand petals.
That will do for a place to sit.
Sitting there you will have a glimpse
of beauty inside the body.
And out of it before gardens and after gardens.
Kabir

What do we mean by the power of breath?

This is breathing in a way that puts you at the center
of yourself. It is the first step in learning to meditate,
and get in touch with the needs of your soul,
or higher self.

How can it benefit me?

You can use breathing techniques to control pain, focus on
a problem, to de-stress, and and for creative visualization.

How do I start?

Begin by taking deep breathes from your diaphragm, rather
than the upper chest, then follow the meditation outlined
in this chapter.

We all breathe, every minute of every day of our lives, yet this action, which
brings life to our bodies, can also nourish our souls. Understanding the power
of breath, and learning to use your breathing positively, is your gateway to
successful meditation and all the benefits it brings.

Breathing is like carrying around a personal barometer that shows what's going on beneath the skin.

Breathing and meditation

The first and last things we do with our bodies while we are here on earth concerns the breath. It is literally our inspiration for life when we arrive. When we breathe our last breath, then life is over.

Breathing is just one of the millions of things that go on all by themselves in our bodies moment by moment, year in, year out. But breathing has other applications besides transporting clean and dirty air in and out of your nostrils. Becoming aware of how you breathe opens up more than the alveoli in your lungs. It can become a vital aid on the journey of "becoming."

Becoming aware of our breath not only keeps us alive in the world of the five senses, but is also a key to experiencing life from a deeper, wider, and fuller perspective of consciousness. Once we become aware of how our breathing is involved not simply in staying alive, but being alive in a more conscious way, we can use it as a vital tool to access our inner world. Using the breath, we can get in touch with the stillness that is always there beneath the choppy and turbulent waters of everyday life.

This freely available commodity can supplement our wellbeing and become the way to a healthier body, mind, and soul.

How your body breathes

Have you ever watched a baby breathe? Its little diaphragm moves rhythmically and peacefully (when it is asleep), using all of its tiny lungs to re-oxygenate its blood, its abdomen looking like a balloon expanding and contracting. Now go and have a look in the mirror, and watch yourself breathe. What happens to your shoulders? Do they look as if they are attached to your ears in some invisible way? Does the air ever get a chance to go right down to your belly? A baby breathes naturally and freely, but as soon as life begins to thrust into its awareness, its breathing will become shallow and restricted by the fears and anxieties it will encounter. Our breathing is greatly influenced by our moods. Our minds can become reactive and agitated when the outside environment is not calm and peaceful. Our attention is occupied with what might happen in the future, or what has happened in the past. Our bodies suffer from the effects of our attention always being focused on what is happening around us, and never on what is going on within us.

Each emotion and significant thought has an associated breathing pattern. When we become stressed, anxious or fearful we breathe in shallow, rapid breaths—sometimes hardly breathing at all. This is the body's response to having the fight-or-flight button pressed. We might heave a sigh of relief when the tension has passed, which is the cue for the body to relax again, but most of the time we just

We use our breath to hold down or control feelings that we do not want to release.

increase the tension. This means we become used to breathing with only the top part of our lungs, so our body suffers. Our hearts get stressed, we cannot digest food properly, our blood does not get fully oxygenated, and we remain in a state of emotional tension. We use our breath, too, to hold down or control feelings that we do not want to release.

Stop right now, put one hand on your upper chest and the other hand on your belly. Close your eyes and think of a recent situation that made you feel upset or agitated. Pay attention to which of your hands is moving in response to your breathing.

Now let the memory of that situation dissolve. Bring to mind a situation, a place, or event where you feel calm and glad to be alive. Notice any difference?

The mind connection

How could breathing possibly affect our minds? It is only too easy to allow our minds to become our masters. Circling, repetitive thoughts lead to furrowed brows, tension, and anxiety in the solar plexus. It has been said somewhere that we think over 30,000 thoughts a day and 75 per cent of those thoughts we thought yesterday! Not the most creative use of an incredibly sophisticated piece of equipment. We can get ourselves into a state of fear and resistance at the drop of a hat. Stuck in a traffic jam, our minds can give us a major production about the consequences of being late. Tense and anxious, we stay stuck in the jam. Thinking about doing your income tax returns or writing that letter, making that phone call or doing something that you are dreading can encourage

your mind to produce endless excuses, or come up with worst-case scenarios. By doing some conscious breathing, you can shift the frame of reference and choose what you want to think.

Just take a breath in, and then let a big sigh out. Say to yourself. "I breathe in … and I breathe out … I breathe in peace and I breathe out tension." Just focusing on breathing in peace, and breathing out tension for a few moments allows the mental static to calm, and you can then think in a more positive, useful way. Practice conscious breathing in moments of thought-induced stress, fear or anxiety, and notice what happens.

Breathing and your soul

Perhaps we might say that the soul is like the axis of a wheel. Each spoke of the wheel represents an aspect of your personality, a role you play or a mask you wear. There may be many spokes to your wheel—parent, career person, dreamer, DIYer, organizer, company director, gardener, procrastinator, artist, or whatever.

Stop and think of a few of the spokes that make up your wheel. You might want to draw a wheel in your journal and write in the aspects of your personality that represent each spoke.

Yes, you are all of these people (Carl Jung called them "sub-personalities"), but there is "One behind" all of these roles—parent or businessman—the nature of the One behind remains constant. By becoming aware of that One behind, we can play all our different parts in a more soul-full way and this is where breathing comes in. Conscious breathing is the key to connecting with that still, small voice

In Buddhism, the aim of meditation is to get beyond the practical voice in your head that prevents you drifting into a meditative state. If you achieve this, it is known as attaining the "Buddha self."

that cannot be heard above the cacophony of sound that fills our daily lives. All your different roles may be played with the guidance that is found at the axis of your wheel. When you feel you are getting too caught up in one of your roles, conscious breathing will remind you of the central axis of the wheel—that place where you have a wider, wiser perspective.

Of course we all have thoughts (30,000 a day), but we are not those thoughts. We have emotions too, but we are not those emotions. We also have a body, but neither are we our bodies. The mind thinks, the emotions feel, and the body senses—the soul simply "knows." There is a way to tune into that "knowing" that goes beyond the other aspects of our being, and the door to that way is the breath.

So, apart from being a key to becoming more aware of who you really are, you will also be doing your body a great favor by

> *He who looks outside, dreams;*
> *who looks inside, wakes.*
> C.J. Jung

learning how to breathe more fully. You will be able to consciously influence your thoughts and feelings and make considered responses to situations instead of reactive ones. The wonderful Vietnamese Buddhist, Thich Nhat Hanh, calls this approach to life "mindfulness"—being in the moment—which is a powerful place to be.

To further convince you of the need to pay more attention to what is happening between your nostrils and your lungs, consider the following uses to which you might put your breath.

Soul focus

Breathing is the key to peace and stillness. In peace and stillness we may hear the soul.

✳

Paying attention to your breathing calms your mind, your body, and emotions.

✳

Taking a few deep conscious breaths puts you in the axis of your wheel.

✳

Use your breathing to keep your awareness in the moment. Being in the moment means you have a choice about what you want to think and feel.

✳

Breathing with your belly brings balance.

BUILDING UP ENERGY Breath can energize the body by building a "charge" that is created using sharp inhalation and exhalation techniques. Known as the "Breath of Fire" by yogis.

DIRECTING ATTENTION Breathing can help us focus and direct attention to a specific part of ourselves. This is useful for helping pain and discomfort.

ACCESSING INFORMATION Controlled breathing allows us to gain information from the unconscious mind more easily.

ALTERING THOUGHTS AND FEELINGS Changing the way we breathe allows us to change our thoughts and feelings. By changing the pattern of our breathing, we can make a conscious decision on how we wish to respond to a situation. Taking a deep breath in a tense situation helps us to keep calm.

*How we breathe reveals the state we're in. Our breathing pattern
alters according to whether we feel withdrawn, euphoric, or anxious.
In this way, breathing helps us release or suppress emotions.*

REFLECTING ON THOUGHTS AND FEELINGS
By observing our breathing patterns, we can
become aware of the effects on our body
of certain thoughts and feelings.

CHANGING CONSCIOUSNESS Controlled
breathing techniques are used in some
meditation practices and certain forms of
therapy to induce a shift to non-ordinary
states of consciousness.

**LINKING TOGETHER THE CONSCIOUS AND
THE UNCONSCIOUS MIND** Breathing provides
a gateway between the conscious mind and
the physiological functions that are generally
controlled by the unconscious body-mind.

Yes, there is more to breathing than meets
the eye. Becoming aware of it brings you right
into the here-and-now, and deep, centered
breathing—which means breathing from your
belly, not your upper chest—immediately
anchors you in your body in a fundamental
awareness of the rhythmic flow of life.

Breathing and meditation

But what has breathing to do with meditation? Paying attention only to the air coming in and out of your nostrils begins the process of taking your attention away from the outside world, to investigate what might be going on in your inside world. And as we turn inward (for we are surely not going to find our souls out there), the first thing we need to do is to respectfully ask the left brain to take time off (which it does not always agree to do) so that we can listen to the other side of the story. We need to lose our mind and come to our senses, and from there we can move beyond the issues of right and wrong (or left), black and white, good and bad, into that place where there is no judgment, no words—only experience.

The differences between the left and right sides of your brain were covered in the last chapter, and it is important to remember that meditation has absolutely nothing to do with the left brain. Millions of words have been written on the subject of meditation, and there are possibly the same number of ways of getting to the same place. The thing to remember is that it is not about doing anything.

Some meditation practices focus on the seven chakra points on the body, known as energy wheels. The Third Eye chakra, shown here, is the second chakra.

Meditation is a state of being. We have become accomplished human doings (left brain again). What is it like to be a human "Being"?

Meditation puts us in touch with our soul. We experience a distinct change in the whole atmosphere and vibration of our body. It is as if the body dissolves as our focus becomes internalized. The brain waves slow down from beta (the level of wakeful, decision-making consciousness) to alpha, which is the frequency of light trance and daydreaming. We develop a different perception on the problems of life after we have taken them into meditation—the things that matter and wind us up seem to become less important when they are considered from a place of balance and alignment. This is rather like looking down on an anthill from an eagle's perspective. This place of alignment is sensed only when your body is calm and relaxed and your mind has become still, which is the essence of meditation.

Meditation is not about going to sleep. In meditation, the body is calm and relaxed, the mind is focused and aware. Focused on what? Focused on nothing. "Nothing?" says the left brain. "Impossible! How can you think of nothing?". This is a classic example of the way the left brain sabotages anything that threatens its autonomy, and it will probably try to continue sabotaging by interfering with intrusive, incessant thoughts—just like a child that always wants attention. Buddhists call this state the "monkey mind." When you recognize this as simply the left brain trying to retain its control, you can move away from the struggle of wrestling with these thoughts, and just wait for them to settle.

Our left brain function is essential for survival in the physical world and you will probably find that it has difficulty, at first, in letting go. It insists on popping thoughts into the important spaces that you are creating. Space and nothingness are anathema to the left brain, and this is where conscious breathing is

your ally. In fact, you have two allies to help you focus on nothing: breathing is one of them, and the other is your posture.

It may be possible to meditate in a crumpled heap, and also lying down, but it is more effective when you become aware of yourself "sitting straight like a mountain." First, find a chair that supports your back and is reasonably comfortable. Your feet need to be on the ground with no crossed legs, and with your hands resting on your thighs. Or you might prefer to use the traditional yogi position of

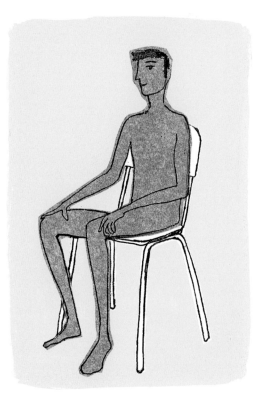

For meditative breathing, sit upright with a straight back and arms placed loosely on the thighs with feet firmly on the floor.

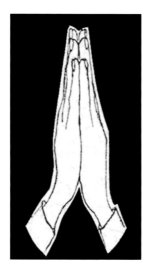

When you have finished your meditation, it is important to say "Thank you." This can be to the universe, or to your chosen deity. This ritual closes the meditation.

sitting on a cushion or meditation stool with your legs folded in front of you. How might it feel to be a mountain? Sitting squarely on your bottom, close your eyes, and imagine that there is a string coming from the top of your head, connecting you to an unseen point above it. Allow your backbone to align with this. Drop your chin a fraction—your head will know where to find the right position. You can then begin to become aware of your breathing. All you have to do is notice the breath moving in and out of your nostrils—this is the beginning of taking your attention inward. Just breathing, and knowing that you are breathing. That is all.

As your attention begins to let go of the external world, you may begin to notice which parts of your body are holding tension.

Now the body is being taken care of, the next area that will need—probably even demand—attention will be the mind. Meditation has nothing to do with the process of logical, rational thought, so remember that your left brain will probably feel uncomfortable about a shift in the power base. This is natural. The best approach is not to create conflict with the mind, but to allow it to think its thoughts and do the "monkey mind" bit—filling the space with ceaseless chatter. Can you imagine you are

What lies behind us and what lies before us are tiny matters
Compared with what lies within us.
Oliver Wendell Holmes

the observer of your thoughts? Let the mind settle itself. Imagine watching a stream that has become stirred up and muddy—to try and make the stream clearer, you do not jump in, you just sit on the bank and wait. There is nothing to be done, because whatever you do will make it more muddy. Just watch and wait.

As your thoughts settle themselves, start to be aware of how your mind works. The moment you become aware of the functioning of your mind, you realize that you are not the mind and that very awareness means you have gone beyond the mind—you have become the witness. You no longer identify yourself with that thought—you are the thinker of the thought. The more aware you become, the more you will be able to see the gaps between the experience and the words—between two words there is always a gap, a silence. Between two notes of music there is always a gap, a silence. That silence is always there, but you do have to be aware and attentive to feel it. The more aware you become, then the slower the mind becomes. The less aware you are, the faster the mind is. It is always relative.

Heightened awareness means that the mind slows down, and the gaps between all your thoughts widen. As you come to understand the subtle workings of your mind, a great awareness wells up in you, which is not of the mind. That awareness arises in your being, in your soul, in your consciousness.

Meditation is sometimes referred to as a state of nothingness, or no-thing-ness. So, sitting like a mountain, with your body relaxed and calm, just noticing your breath move gently in and out through your nostrils, you become the observer of your thoughts.

All schools of meditation state the need for consciousness to be focused between and behind the eyes. This is the location of the pineal gland, and is the position of the Third Eye or Brow chakra—the center associated with insight, intuition and inner vision. It is also knows as "the throne of the soul" or "gateway to the void." It is an appropriate place to review events and issues with the eye that sees in all directions, without judgment and with the clarity that comes from that one still voice.

In some meditation practice, the sound of Tibetan singing bowls emits a spiritual harmonic which helps induce deep relaxation.

Meditation techniques

There are many different routes to the same destination and you need to find the one most suitable for you. Some people find it easier and a more powerful experience to meditate with others in a group. You may prefer it to be a solitary experience. Whatever you choose is really only a training for approaching every moment of life as a meditation.

Centering prayer

This form of meditation uses the focus of a word or phrase of your choice. The energy of the words themselves shifts awareness from the clouds to the sky itself, encouraging a meditative state and a change in perception. Think of prayer words such as: Peace, Love, Thank You, I am, Compassion—whatever word inspires you to an awareness of a power that is greater than yourself—the Divine Presence. Then you can let go of the word and just sit quietly, letting the quality, the sense of the word infuse the space.

Holy moment meditation

After you have gone through the preparation of posture, breathing and body relaxation, bring to mind the memory of one of those moments when you felt a deep sense of "connection." Perhaps it was a sunset, the smile of a baby, a view from a cliff top or a special moment with a loved one. Involve all your senses in this recollection. Remembering how that sense of being connected infused your whole being. Then let the memory go and meditate on the feelings that remain—those feelings of being connected to and part of something that is so much more.

*Incense is a meditation aid, used by many religious and non-religious
practices to create calm space for prayer or meditation.*

Walking meditation

Sometimes our minds just will not settle down, especially if there has been some bad news or there is a major event on the horizon, in which case you might like to try the practice of the walking meditation that has been popularized by Thich Nhat Hanh, the Buddhist monk mentioned earlier. Find somewhere quiet to walk, preferably in natural surroundings, although it works on pavements too. Begin by focusing on your breathing. Then notice the movements of your feet—see how your lift each one, moving forward in space, and then bring it down again. Then let your awareness expand beyond the physical sensation of walking, to the environment around you, keeping 25 per cent of your awareness on your breathing and 75 per cent on a spacious awareness of everything you see, hear, feel and smell. If your mind kicks in, let go of your thoughts, and return to an awareness of your breathing and each movement of your feet, taking you back into mindfulness.

Music and dancing meditation

Rave and hip-hop music may induce certain kinds of altered states, but you are more likely to be receptive to communications from your soul when in a still and peaceful space. You might have a favorite piece of music that transports you. If not there is plenty available, from Gregorian chant, Tibetan bowls, didgeridoo, an exquisite piece of Bach, Mozart, or anything that doesn't have lyrics to engage the mind and allows you to enter the sound. Dance is another way to lose your mind and come to your senses, as any whirling Sufi dervish could tell you. Dance can provide you with the river on which to sail out to the wider sea.

Soul focus

Meditation makes the space for experiencing connection to your soul.

✳

The more you practice meditation, the easier it becomes to
open to soul-fullness.

✳

Make meditation part of your daily routine—even if sometimes you can
only manage 10 minutes. Five minutes of mindful meditation is more valuable
than 50 minutes of mental wandering.

✳

Make a space to meditate that is sacred. Light a candle, or put a flower in
a vase. A ritual, however seemingly insignificant, marks a rite of passage
between two states of being. Make sure you will not be interrupted. Take your
phone off the hook. Even yogis find it difficult to meditate at a railway station.

✳

Try different methods of meditation until you find one that suits you: following
the notes of music can take you into spaciousness; focusing on the flame
of your candle might be a way that takes you within; sitting with your back
to a tree, or under the stars or anywhere in nature, just breathing and being
aware, may also open up your sense of connection. Make sure you are not too
tired when you begin your meditation practice, and also not too warm and
comfortable, or you'll go to sleep.

✳

If you are in emotional pain or turmoil, you cannot get outside to do the
Walking meditation, and it seems impossible to sit and be still because your
thoughts and feelings just seem to intensify, then perhaps it is time to just
notice how much time is spent running away from anxieties and uncomfortable
feelings. Sticking with it, and allowing yourself the time and space to really feel
the emotions, transforms the fear that we will be overwhelmed by them.

✳

Don't try too hard! It is about becoming a human "Being."

CHAPTER 3

The Aura and the Universal Energy Field

What is an aura?

An aura is a personal energy field. Everything that exists has an aura, but life force creates a stronger aura, which is why a human or insect will have a stronger aura than that of a desk or a book.

How can an awareness of auras benefit me?

By becoming sensitive to the vibrations, or auras, of yourself and others you can learn to sense people who drain you of energy, and recognize those who give you energy.

How can I work with my aura?

You can learn to cleanse your aura of negative static from others, which gives you renewed energy and a better understanding of your emotions.

If you were able to see your aura, you would see a pulsating, shimmering energy field surrounding your body. Observed by mystics, artists, and healers through the ages, it was described by the Pythagoreans of ancient Greece as a "luminous" body, a light body. Everything that has an atomic structure has an energy field, so everything from a pea to a planet will have an aura. Because the energy of animated life is more vibrant, it is easier to sense the energy field of a chipmunk than that of a chair.

Before going into more detail about the nature of your own personal aura, it is useful to put it into a wider context. Like the student fish that asks its teacher: "What is this sea that people talk about?", we swim about in a space that supports and nourishes us and connects us with everything else in the sea. This sea that we find ourselves in, is called the universal energy field. It is a vast ocean of energy that radiates in all directions. It is the ultimate information highway. Your link to this, your computer or telephone, is already installed—it is just a matter of activating the line. Everything we can see and touch, taste, and hear begins its life in this field of energy. Every thing in existence was first an idea. How else could it come into being? Even the paper on which you are reading these words was first an idea in someone's mind, or it could not have materialized.

The aura, or energy field of a willow tree helps banish a headache; pine is a natural cleanser, purifying negative energy, and oak trees create a sense of support and strength.

Sense beyond reason

Einstein proved that energy and matter are interchangeable. Matter is simply energy that has slowed down. Forms are built from energy, they collapse and then re-form. Empirical science says we must believe only what can be proved, the result of this thinking is an extremely limited, uninspired world view. Our own ability to perceive the world we live in is also limited. For a start, we know that our perception of color and sound is restricted to a narrow band. There are ultraviolet and infrared bands on either end of our visible color spectrum which we cannot see, and sounds which animals can hear that we cannot. Our senses have become dulled, we are no longer in tune with the world in which we live. Even at the most basic level, we are often unaware of what our own bodies are trying to tell us when they express disease.

The universal energy field, the ocean in which we consciously exist, stores all information. Carl Jung, the psychologist, visionary and father of modern psychotherapy, called this the collective unconscious. Dr Rupert Sheldrake, a Cambridge biologist, believes that this infinite library is made up of what he calls morphogenic fields, or pockets of information. When enough individuals have accessed the information from one of these fields of consciousness, or libraries, it becomes available to all the others. This is sometimes referred to as the

100th Monkey Syndrome. This term was coined after observing monkeys on an island in the southern seas. One of these monkeys, having stolen a yam, inadvertently dropped it in the sea, and noticed that it tasted more delicious without earth on it. Others in the troupe began to follow suit. The remarkable thing was that before long, troupes of monkeys on the other islands also began to wash their stolen yams. How had they managed to get hold of this information? The theory is that when a sufficient number of the original troupe of monkeys were washing their yams, it created a field of information. When this field had reached critical mass, it enabled all the other monkeys everywhere simultaneously to know what to do. This theory helps explain such phenomena as simultaneous scientific breakthroughs—the discovery of DNA, for example, by different scientists in different parts of the world within days of one another. It is also an exciting prospect from the point of view of consciousness in general. When enough of us work on remembering who we are, on raising the level of our own consciousness, then that information becomes available for everyone. Nothing ever happens in isolation, because everything is interconnected. There is order and chaos, movement, and rhythm all around us.

The rhythm of life

Stop for just for a moment and think about the rhythms that go on all around you, and also within you. Birth, life, and death of cells and bodies, the days, months, and seasons; everything moves in cycles. The moon affects not only the tides, but all of life on our planet—including us. The earth and planets move around the sun, the solar system in turn has its own precise cyclical movement—everything occurs in precise order. In our own bodies there are rhythms and cycles that move in time with one another. We do not stand outside the laws and principles that govern the entire cosmos; there is an implicate order to everything. Primitive cultures such as the Aborigines and bushmen understood these laws and rhythms and lived in accordance with them.

Our preoccupation with the material world has led us away from the knowledge that we are part of a much wider whole. We have ignored these laws and put ourselves, as well as our planet, in peril. Nature is abundant—it always makes too much! By using the power and energy of the Natural Laws instead of trying to conquer everything, that abundance is available for us, too.

Becoming aware of ourselves as part of the living universe, both visible and invisible, gives us a different perspective, and requires a paradigm shift. So let us see (or rather, sense) what we can find out about our own energy field, remembering that it operates within a vast moving sea of information and energy.

We receive vital, life-sustaining nourishment from this energy source. In India it is referred to as *prana*, in China as *chi*. T'ai chi and Qi gong are exercise movements that encourage the free flow of this life force into and around our physical beings. It is important to encourage this free flow, because we are no different from our own planet, whose energy field, or aura, has now become congested, punctured, and contaminated with negative human emissions, both physical and mental.

What is an aura?

Something like a halo surrounding the whole body, the aura is like a cloak of moving colors around every individual. The colors the aura shows vary according to your physical health and also depending on what you are thinking and feeling. Remember the expressions "going green with envy," "seeing red," or "feeling blue"? Your aura is made up of several levels, known as bodies. It is something like a Russian doll, except that each layer interacts with and interpenetrates the others. Being aware of the interaction between your body, thoughts, and feelings means there will be a freer flow of energy between the different levels, or frequencies, that make up your subtle anatomy.

Each body, or level, has a different vibration, going from the physical body which has the slowest frequency and is the densest, to the outer levels of the auric field which are much finer and have a faster vibration. These subtle bodies alter according to what goes on inside us. They reflect the state of our body, our feelings, our minds, and our spiritual development.

They are also affected by what goes on outside. Environmental stress: noise, pollution, and electromagnetic fields (VDUs, overhead cables, underwater streams, geopathic stress, and radio and satellite transmitters) affect our auric field and may result in physical disease.

Our auras reflect the state we are in. They protect us, they nourish us, and the health of our subtle anatomy affects the health of our physical body. When we are in love with life, our energy field expands and is vibrant. When we feel down and depressed, however, it becomes gray and contracted. The auric field of an alcoholic suffering from depression will look murky, depleted, and might have rents or holes in it. On the other hand, the aura of someone like the Dalai Lama is extended, clear, and sparkling with his humor and spirituality.

How do you know that you have an aura?

If you answer "yes" to any of the following questions, then you have experienced the interplay of an outside energy field upon your own:

When you are with certain people, do you feel drained?

✳

Do you associate certain colors with people?

✳

Have you ever "felt" someone staring at you?

✳

Have you ever taken an instant liking or disliking to someone?

✳

Are you able to sense how someone is feeling, in spite of how this person is behaving?

✳

Have you been able to sense another person's presence before you actually saw or heard this person?

✳

Do certain colors and sounds make you feel more comfortable than others?

✳

Do you feel the "vibes" in a place when you enter it?

✳

Can you "sense" when something is wrong?

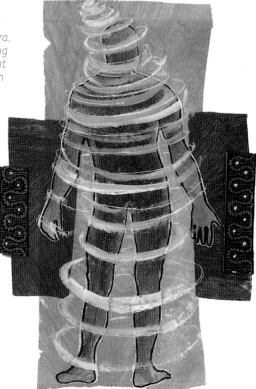

Whenever you encounter another person, you come into contact with their aura. As energy flows from strong to weak, you may find that some people feed you with energy, whereas others deplete you.

By becoming aware of your own auric field, you will begin to notice how it interacts with outside forces and energies. You begin to notice how you affect, and are affected by, the energy of others. You need to be aware of those times when it is important to strengthen, balance, and cleanse this energy.

DRAINS AND RADIATORS You need to be aware of the situations and people that "drain" you, and what it is that makes you radiant. Another point to remember is that energy always flows from strong to weak. We talk about being in tune with another person, being on the same frequency—these are the people who resonate with our own frequency, who are on the same wavelength. But we do not always find ourselves with this type of person. You therefore need to become sensitive to how your energy can get drained away by others. Every time you come in contact with another person, two energy fields meet and, because of the electromagnetic properties of the aura, this encounter may result in you giving energy (the electrical aspect) or alternatively absorbing energy (the magnetic aspect). The more people you interact with, the greater the energy exchange. Unless you are aware of this exchange, you can accumulate debris that is not yours by the end of the day, making you feel drained and washed out.

NATURAL ENERGIZERS On the plus side, being in nature is both balancing and cleansing. Fresh air, the scent of grass, and stimulus of an ocean or stream all give immediate benefits. Trees have a particularly dynamic energy field and, just as with each human being, every tree has its own unique frequency. Sitting under a willow tree, for example, helps get rid of a headache. Pine trees have a particularly cleansing effect as they help to draw off negative emotions, and an oak tree will offer you strength and support.

Now let us have a look at the first four bodies that make up our subtle anatomy, or auric field. There are more levels beyond these four, but it is important to begin at the beginning, and really understand the basics first.

The first level of the aura, which extends just beyond the physical body, is known as the etheric double, or template. Then comes the astral body, then the mental body and then the causal, or soul, body.

Think about the people with whom you have felt truly uplifted. These individuals are "radiators," who literally radiate positive energy which can be seen or sensed in the aura.

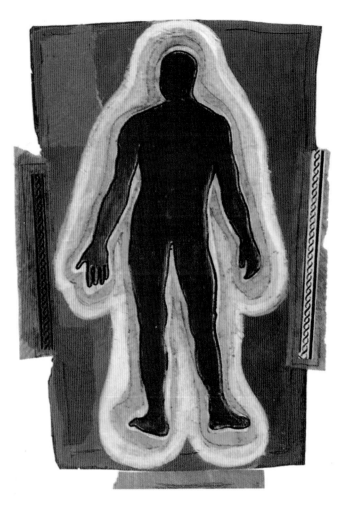

The aura is formed like a layered egg. Its energy is more dense in the layers closest to the physical body.

The etheric body

Being the closest to the physical, this is the first of the subtle bodies which may be sensed. To those who are able to see it, it looks like a misty material which projects just out from the physical body, or it may be felt, especially with your hands. It is composed of matter vibrating at speeds just above the velocity of light, which makes it invisible to our everyday senses. In 1939 a Russian called Senyon Kirlian discovered a method of "photographing" this energy body, which showed that there is an energy blueprint, or matrix, from which every living thing develops. When a leaf is photographed using this method, it shows an outline of energy emanations. If part of the leaf is cut off and then it is photographed again, the whole outline of the leaf re-appears. This is known as the phantom leaf effect, and accounts for many people who have had limbs amputated still experiencing sensation in a part of their body that no longer physically exists. What is also interesting about this method of photography is that disease can be detected as a low emanation of energy at this level, even before it manifests itself in the physical body.

Our souls require a human body to collect experience on earth. There is not much point in being an angel if you need to work out a control issue with your mother-in-law.

So, in order to come into this human form and to experience what it has contracted to experience, our souls choose the body and parents that will offer the opportunities it requires. This is like choosing a car, or even a camel, that has the qualities and characteristics required for particular experiences this time around. Since the souls do not judge experience as being either good or bad, living life driving a clapped-out station wagon is just as valid as gliding around in a beautiful, smooth convertible.

The etheric body is the matrix for the physical form. It is also the interface between matter and non-matter. Try this energy-sensing exercise for yourself:

Energy-sensing exercise

Sit comfortably in a chair, with your palms facing one another,
but not quite touching. Slowly move your palms away from each other.

✳

Then bring them together. Establish a gentle rhythm, moving together,
then apart as though there were an invisible elastic band between them.
You might notice that it feels as if you are holding something.
You may begin to feel an energy field build up between your hands.

✳

Just close your eyes and breathe in an even, relaxed way.
Notice how far apart you can take your hands before you lose
the sense of the ball of energy that you have created.

The astral or emotional body

The next level, which projects out further than the etheric double, has a finer vibration and is called the astral body. This body follows the Law of Attraction which means that, through our emotions, we will attract towards us all that is needed for our soul's experience and growth. Whereas the etheric body "senses" things, this level of our aura "feels."

Every feeling we experience has a different energy charge. Feeling depressed has a different frequency, obviously, from a current of anger. We metabolize these feelings as we metabolize a plate of pasta—they are turned into something else. Our feelings register on the astral body of our aura. Compassion and unconditional love, joy, peace, and purposefulness will make your aura look and feel quite different from the charge of fear, guilt, anger, and hate. All feelings need to be felt and expressed (appropriately) otherwise they become held in the auric field and metastasize into blocks, or pockets of stuck energy that will prevent the normal free flow around us. Continuing to suppress or hold on to these feelings over a period of time will then affect the etheric body and finally impact on the cells in our physical body, which will begin to express this congestion as disease. Understanding the connection between thoughts and feelings and their effect on our bodies is now becoming the recognized branch of medicine already referred to as PNI.

Because the vibrations of the astral body are finer than our dense physical form, we can travel at will in this body—hence the term astral travel. We all enter the astral plane when we sleep. Here we can meet up with other souls and travel to places which would be difficult to reach in our everyday life. Some healers do a great deal of work using their astral bodies, which accounts for reports of healers appearing in their patients' homes at all times of the day or night, and also appearing to them in their dreams. Many other people have experienced OBEs (out-of-body-experiences) which often happen spontaneously, but can also be consciously induced. These experiences

Some of the challenges presented to us at the level of the astral body are:

✳

Over-identification with our emotions (we have emotions, but we are not those emotions).

✳

Under-identification with or suppression of our emotions ("I don't want to feel this").

✳

Identification with the desires of the personality rather than the soul—losing connection with the axis of your wheel.

✳

often go hand-in-hand with an opening of the psychic faculty. For more information on this, and also psychic protection, Judy Hall's excellent book, *The Art of Psychic Protection*, is recommended.

The mental or causal body

This is the body that is the starting point for the soul to integrate its intelligence with that of the body. It is where the impulses of the soul or higher self become thought forms, which are then transformed into action. These thought forms may come during sleep, in the form of dreams, during meditation, or they may slowly develop as an idea that enters the conscious mind as something that needs to be done. If we operate at this level without paying attention to the presence of the soul, everything is seen as black or white, right or wrong. This is the left brain in cahoots with our ego, believing that there is only a three-dimensional reality and a needing to feel safe. From this limited perspective, we will respond to situations according to what we have filed away in our memory banks under the heading of Belief Systems. These belief systems, about who we are and how we should behave, may be appropriate for our development, or they may be scripts carried forward from our early years that become like tapes that have got looped in our systems. "Could do better," "It's not safe to trust people," "I'll never have enough," "Men always let you down," are examples of the negative, restricting myths that we are often quite unaware of and which prevent us from living life to the full. The lower levels of the mental body are concerned with rational,

Logical thought, such as mathematical problem-solving, is the realm of the lower mental body.

logical thought while the higher levels are responsible for abstract, intuitive thinking.

Try this imaging exercise lying in bed before you go to sleep at night, to clear any unwanted static that you may have collected during the day. It is particularly useful if you have been in an environment where another person, with whom you are in close contact, seems to be affecting you in a negative way and depleting your energy. You may like to record it.

Waterfall cleansing exercise

I focus on my breathing, taking some deep, easy breaths.

✳

I imagine, or get a sense of a beautiful, crystal-clear waterfall splashing down.

✳

The water has a diamond-like quality to it.

✳

Now I imagine that I am standing underneath this waterfall. It is going right through
my auric field, taking with it any slow-frequency energy, any blocks of static
that I might have accumulated during the day.

✳

Its clarity and refreshing coolness feel invigorating and refreshing.

✳

Now I imagine that this water enters in through the top of my head.

✳

It goes right through my body and out through the ends of my
fingers and toes.

✳

I notice that the water coming out from my toes and fingers might seem cloudy and dark.

✳

So I continue to allow the water to move through me until the color coming
out through my toes and fingers is as clear as the waterfall itself.

✳

When this has happened, I then imagine that I am filling my inner space with
this water—clear and clean, invigorating and revitalizing.

✳

Now I step out from under the waterfall and find a white cloak or coat that is there for me.
By putting this on, and wrapping it around me ensures that my personal space is protected
from invasion. I take a deep breath, wriggle my fingers and toes and then open my eyes.

✳

The soul or causal body

Extending further out now from the physical "yolk" and the previous three bodies that make up our aura is the soul body. This vibrates at a level far beyond the frequencies so far described. At this level we do not sense, feel, or think—we just know. This body carries the information and imprints of many lifetimes— experiences that have been significant enough to make their mark on us. Dying with a powerful thought or feeling—betrayal, for example—may be carried forward into the next lifetime as an echo of that event. This may be experienced as an unconscious and possibly unfounded mistrust of people.

Without wanting to reduce the soul by using modern technological terms to describe it, we could say that it is like a disc in a computer. Information is put in and stored. We remove it. We want to work with that material again. Some of the events recorded may not be a true expression of who we are, so we edit and re- write it. If we do not live our lives under the guidance from this level, the disc will continue to be overlayed with the desires of the three lower bodies. Since the soul lives outside linear time and space, the number of lifetimes it takes to remember how it is to be a soul in human form is of no consequence. It will remember. There is always free will and choice.

Thankfully, the soul has an ally for its work, and that ally is the heart. As the soul body is the interface between the divine and physical reality, so it is with the heart. Heartfelt actions are not directed by mental or astral bodies, thoughts, or feelings—they have a different quality to them. We are in search of meaning. For many, organized religions do not offer the key to re-connection or re-collection of soulfulness. We are leaving the Age of Pisces, which has been about personal power and control, "I believe, therefore I experience" has been the maxim for the last 2,000-year period. Now we have arrived at the Age of Aquarius which says "I experience, therefore I believe." In other words, our own personal, direct experience of that otherness that is the quality of soul—this is what matters. Following doctrines and creeds, unless we have had experience of soul, is like reading a map without trying to explore the territory itself.

Soul focus

Our bodies, feelings, and thoughts are the means for our soul's experience.

✳

Becoming aware that you are more than your physical body enables you to perceive the finer vibrations of your soul.

✳

Here is the next visualization exercise to record for yourself. It will help keep your energy contained and focused, and prevent any drains or leeches from helping themselves to your energy and depleting your power source. After recording it on a tape, make yourself comfortable in a chair that supports your back. Sit in it with a straight spine, and then take some deep, easy breaths, letting go of tension with each exhalation...

Auric egg visualization

Take some deep, easy breaths to help you let go of tension.
Then mentally think:

✳ I release the tension in my feet, my legs, my abdomen, my chest, my
arms and hands, my neck, and head. I imagine, or get a sense that I am
sitting in an egg, this egg is light and goes all the way round me. It is my
energy field, I can control this egg of energy that is around me, but first
I need to become aware of how it can be affected not only by what goes
on around it, but also by what goes on inside it.

✳ Being aware of this energy egg around me, I just allow my mind to
think for a moment of a recent experience that I didn't particularly enjoy.
I notice how I felt during that experience, and now I notice what has
happened to my egg. Now I think for a moment of a recent experienced
that warmed my heart, and notice what happens to my egg. Becoming
aware of this auric egg of mine means I can contract or expand it at will.

✳ I will now check the health of my egg. I imagine I am in the center
of it, my physical body is the yolk, the densest part of an egg, and it is
a golden white color. Around this yolk is the white and this is the space
which I want to be clean and clear, without any static, strings, cords,
or any other bits and pieces. I imagine clear colors here such as blue,
silver, or gold. Around these colors is a delicate skin or membrane and
surrounding this is the shell. Under a microscope I can see that this shell
is semi-permeable, in fact energy can move in and through it, but it also
protects the vulnerable contents. I have a look inside the shell to see if

any parts of it need repair work, if there are any holes or parts
that appear damaged. I will mend or repair them in whatever way
feels appropriate.

✳ Now I take a look around the outside and see that there is a buffer
zone surrounding me, like a lavender-colored piece of foam rubber.
When I have got a sense of these fields or levels that surround me,
I go back into the awareness of the center, the golden yolk of my egg.
Now I imagine that I am floating out on a silver cord into the wider
space beyond. I am safe and protected as I explore a little further, my
silver cord keeps me in contact with my egg as I imagine myself floating
deeper, further, into this space—this outer space which is the same
as inner space, traveling past many life experiences, through the past
and the future, out into the timelessness of all things—to a different
state of being.

✳ Inner and outer space melt and fuse into the same experience,
I feel unbounded, an expansive freedom, a horizon so wide and vast,
it becomes no horizon—just the middle of a familiar ocean where
there is a quietness. I listen to the sound of my own stillness now.

✳ In a moment, I will begin to travel back, gently finding myself coming back through time and space, following my silver cord gently back to my egg, moving down the cord into the golden center of my egg. I become aware once again of the boundary of my egg, with its buffer zone, knowing that this is my own personal, protected space, and I am safe within it. I take a deep breath and become aware of my feet on the floor and my connection to the Earth. When I feel ready, I will start to move my toes and fingers and then slowly open my eyes.

NOTE

Practice the Auric egg meditation regularly. Use it before going into an energy-threatening situation. Express your feelings. Don't stuff them away to metastasize into disease. If they are feelings you are afraid of (such as anger), write it down, bash a pillow but get it out. If it is grief, allow yourself time and space. Forget about the stiff upper lip and allow yourself to plummet the depths. It will be painful, but you won't be overwhelmed.

Become aware of the different levels of experience:

"I sense this is right" (body plus etheric double)

"I feel this is right" (astral and emotional body)

"I think this is right" (mental body)

"I know this is right" (soul body)

Notice how different colors seem to affect you. Practice the Energy-sensing exercise regularly (see page 53) so that your hands become more sensitive and sensitized to energies. Feel the energy that exists around your plants, your cat, and your friends.

CHAPTER 4

The Body Chakras

What is a chakra?

Chakras are the basis of many ancient Eastern healing systems. The seven principal chakras are the seven major power points on the body, from the crown of the head to the genitals.

What are the benefits of chakra healing?

You can pinpoint specific types of physical and emotional health or ill-health through each chakra point. Chakra healers often use a crystal pendulum to dowse over each chakra. The movement of the crystal determines the health of the chakra, and how you may be feeling.

How do I start?

Read through the issues and body symptoms for each chakra, and try the exercises for those you think apply to you just now.

Carl Jung stated that it would take Western culture 100 years to grasp the concept of the chakra system and the subtle anatomy of man. With the explosion in recent years of Eastern practices ranging from acupuncture and t'ai chi to Buddhist meditation and yoga, we are well on our way to achieving that goal well before time. We now have hi-tech equipment that is able to discern the energy meridians used by acupuncturists, the auric field, and the chakra system. A pioneer in this field is an English biologist, Harry Oldfield, who invented electro-crystal therapy as both a diagnostic tool and treatment methodology to rebalance the human energy field.

The chakra system offers a way of understanding the levels of our consciousness from the base, physical levels of survival and reproduction, through to the finer vibrations of insight, intuition and illumination. It is a way of understanding what thoughts and emotions are affecting our physical body and how that comes about. Understanding the functions of the chakras can help us respond to life with awareness, rather than being unconsciously re-active. Each chakra holds the key to help us understand what the soul's sojourn on Earth may be about.

Chakra origins

The word itself is Sanskrit and means "wheel." Chakras are more like spinning energy vortices which are funnel-shaped. The wider, spinning end interacts with our auric field, while the stem appears to be embedded in our spine with a nerve plexus and endocrine gland nearby. We need to understand our chakra system because it has a direct connection with our physical, emotional, and our spiritual wellbeing. Understanding its nature and function can help us respond to life with awareness rather than being unconsciously re-active.

Together, the chakras act as step-down transformers, converting subtle energy—prana or chi—which is then used by the hormonal,

Dowsing over a chakra point with a pendulum reveals the direction in which that chakra spins.

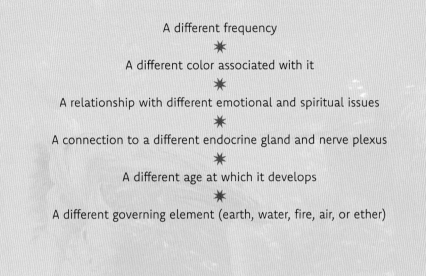

The seven major chakras each have:

A different frequency

✳

A different color associated with it

✳

A relationship with different emotional and spiritual issues

✳

A connection to a different endocrine gland and nerve plexus

✳

A different age at which it develops

✳

A different governing element (earth, water, fire, air, or ether)

nervous, and cellular systems of our body. We take in air and food to fuel our molecular building blocks. The aura and chakras take in the subtle energy, which is also fundamental for life. As well as being linked to the physical functioning of our bodies, each chakra holds a key to understanding our relationships, our strengths and weaknesses, and our sense of who and what we are in the world.

The seven major chakras are aligned with our spinal column, and they are the ones we will be looking at here. There are many other minor ones, from those in the palms of the hands, the soles of the feet, and behind the knees and elbows, to others scattered throughout our body at strategic positions

relevant to the energetic functioning of our physical and etheric bodies.

It is vital to consider the chakras as a whole system, as they affect and interact with one another in a similar way to an orchestra, each chakra having its own "note" to contribute to the symphony. If one of these centers gets out of balance, it affects the others, which try to compensate so that they maintain a state of balance.

The seven chakras are: the Base, Sacral, Solar Plexus, Heart, Throat, Brow, and Crown. We will begin the journey through the chakras starting with the Base chakra.

THE BASE OR ROOT CHAKRA

POSITION: Perineum (central point between the legs)

COLOR: Red

DEVELOPMENTAL AGE: 0—3 years old

ENDOCRINE GLAND: Adrenals

SENSE: Smell

ELEMENT: Earth

CONCERNS: Security, belonging, being here and now, survival

WHEN OUT OF BALANCE: Overly concerned with material security. Jungle mentality.
Being distant. Feeling unsafe, lack of security, no sense of belonging, fear

BODY SYMPTOM: Problems in the rectum and hips. Bowel spasm, piles, colitis,
Crohn's disease, constipation

SOUL ISSUE: To acknowledge that my soul inhabits a body that is part of the living universe.
Through my body my soul is brought into matter for experience in this physical world.
I need to feel safe and present in my body

When we are in the womb our chakra system is as yet not fully developed. Our crown chakra is already open, as it is the connection to where we came from (you can see it in the fontanelle on top of a baby's head). The Base chakra is also open, since we are now coming into human form. The other centers are like little buds on the stem of a flower. These buds will open as we develop into adulthood, and their healthy growth will depend on how we experience life, and our relationship to it.

The Base chakra is affected by how we were greeted at birth, and if approval meant getting love.

The soul takes on human form to learn about life on this earth. There are fundamental rules and regulations that apply to every living thing on the planet and we are no exception. The law of gravity is one example, although the soul is not governed by this law.

We acquire our human body because it is appropriate for the experience required by our soul. We also decide what conditions we need to find ourselves in for soul-learning. Hence we choose our parents—they do not choose us. When we are born, we are open and vulnerable like an open hand, or a soft ball of wax. Life then begins to make its marks on us.

The first and most crucial challenge is to survive, otherwise not much else will happen. The base chakra is concerned with that survival, and the endocrine glands to which it is connected are the adrenals. These are concerned with our "fight or flight" response—a survival mechanism that helps us in life-threatening situations. Not that a baby is going to do much fighting or fleeing, but it is an essential aspect of life on this planet and is probably where the first seeds of fear get imprinted on our soft ball of wax. If, when we arrive, we do not have a welcoming committee—if we are not greeted with loving physical contact (fundamental needs)—we will not feel safe in our little bodies, and the base chakra will not develop in a healthy way. We will not "earth" ourselves, because we do not feel safe, and our soul may not fully connect with our physical being (we would like to keep the options open to going Home, please!). There are many people whose Base chakra has not fully developed because it was simply too scary to find themselves in an early

unsupportive environment. Those born during times of war or conflict (in the home or out of it) will have picked up the vibrations of tension and fear which will wobble their sense of safety at having arrived here. It is often said that being born into life on earth is much more traumatic than dying—which is after all going home.

Having enough of everything

Without this sense of belonging, we build feelings of insecurity, which have unfortunate consequences in later life. To relieve this sense of insecurity, we grow up attached to external sources of security—home, jobs, possessions, and money. Of course it is all right to like nice things, to live in a pleasant environment and have money, but not to rely on these things for our sense of security. Always feeling that there will never be enough to support us makes us feel that we have to acquire more before we can feel safe. These feelings have bred a race of achievers and perfectionists who fear failure, perhaps because they grew up in an environment where being loved was attached to doing well. Even before we learn to speak, we learn that smiling or crying will give us nourishment in one form or another. Born into a situation where there was little nurturing means that we will be afraid to bring our soul energy down to earth.

Questions for the Base chakra

Pause and ask yourself the following questions.
Use your journal to record your thoughts—just write down the first
thing that comes into your mind and trust these insights.

What did it mean to my parents and family when I came into being?

✳

Why did I choose these parents? And this country?

✳

How were the first three years of my life?

✳

Did I feel fearful about my physical wellbeing and survival?

✳

Do I want to be here?

If you feel that your sense of being earthed, or rooted, could do with strengthening, spend more time in nature. Gardening and walking are good ways to connect to the earth. Dancing and drumming help the base center release insecurities. We live in a material world, but we do not have to own everything; think "abundance" instead of "lack." You have everything we need at this moment—it might not be everything you want, but what you have now is exactly what you need. Feeling insecure—consciously or unconsciously—affects the functioning of this chakra, and may produce disease in the body at this level. Panic attacks with palpitations, hyperventilation, frequent visits to the bathroom and muscle spasms are signs of an overactive adrenal gland. Constipation, piles, colitis, diarrhoea, and hypertension are all by-products of fear. Fear of what? That I will not have enough, and therefore I will not survive? That response belongs to the thinking of the inner child.

Go outside, if possible take your shoes off, stand firm upon the earth with knees slightly bent and say: "I am part of the Living Universe. I acknowledge my connection with all living things. In that knowledge I am safe." And say it as if you mean it.

THE SACRAL OR WATER/SEXUAL CHAKRA

POSITION: Just below the navel/the sacrum

COLOR: Orange

DEVELOPMENTAL AGE: 3–5/8 years old

ENDOCRINE GLAND: Reproductive glands—ovaries/testes

SENSE: Taste

ELEMENT: Water

CONCERNS: Intimacy, sharing, child-like mystery, creativity, self-respect

BODY SYMPTOMS: Problems related to the reproductive and urinary systems

SOUL ISSUE: To experience intimacy with another with a sense of self-respect. The expression of creative imagination, in whatever form. The ability to move with the flow of life.

In The Prophet, Kahlil Gibran says, "Give your hearts, but not into each other's keeping." The message of the Sacral chakra is intimacy with self respect.

Having arrived here on earth, our next step is recognizing that we are not alone. The first people that we become aware of are our primary relationships. This is where we learn about relating to one another. How these people behave toward us, and each other, becomes our understanding of "relationship." For many people this is not an encouraging thought! This is why so much therapy takes you back to early childhood in order to identify the old tapes that are looped in our systems. These tapes that were installed when we were little go on repeating unconsciously in adult life, and result in difficult relationships. When we go back into our past and re-live our early frightening experiences, we can collect those aspects of our self that have become frozen in time, believing that there was only one way to respond in order to survive or get love and attention. We may have had a very powerful parent who made it difficult for us to establish our own boundaries. Feeling vulnerable and unsafe, we get sucked into their energy field and have difficulty in establishing our own sense of self. This subject will be gone into in more depth later in the book.

It is also in these early years that we discover that there is a part of our anatomy that gives us lovely feelings—entirely natural for a little person that experiences life totally through its senses. Our parents, however, might have had a different view. What they felt, and expressed, about their sexuality would have a direct effect on how we viewed our own. Another faulty tape may have been installed at this time, saying "That's dirty," "Don't do that, it's naughty," or even worse, "it's disgusting." These days sex has come out of the closet and because of its potent energy is used by marketing moguls to sell everything—shampoo, jeans, telephones—but what about its value as a sacred act?

Creativity and the sacral chakra

The other crucial aspect of the Sacral chakra is to do with creativity (apart from making babies) and the development of our imaginations. When we are small we spend a great deal of time in an imaginary world. We talk to our teddies, who all have their own personalities, and we begin to draw and build things. Stories hold us spellbound as we live the tales of witches and princes, treasure and adventure. Our imaginations are fertile and unfettered. We make up games that have no sense of outcome—we truly live in the moment. We may even have an "imaginary" friend who is a very real presence. We are in touch with magic at this time in our lives. We trust those around us and are open to them. If this trust is ever betrayed, we develop the belief that it is not safe to trust, open up, or be intimate.

Going to school soon changes the focus from the creative use of our imaginations to left-brain skills that are valued so highly in our contemporary culture. Too much television and playing too many computer games shrivels the growth and expression of children's collective imagination. They don't have to invent their own stories because it is done for them. No more fairies found at the bottom of the garden—you'll find them on Channel 3 instead.

So our feelings about sexuality, our relationships with others and our creative

Questions for the Sacral chakra

Using your journal, write the thoughts and insights that come from asking yourself the following questions:

What was the sexual climate like in your home?

✳

What attitudes were expressed towards your developing sexuality?

✳

How do you feel about your sexuality now?

✳

Think about the needs of your inner child—how would it like to express itself?

✳

What did you enjoy doing when you were aged between three and eight?

✳

How do you use your creativity now?

✳

Think of an important relationship in your life. What are you learning?

imagination are formed during this early period of our lives, along with the development of the sacral chakra. If all, or any of these aspects, of our life are knocked out of us, the balance will need to be redressed. The soul speaks through this center with the knowledge that every significant relationship in our lives holds a key to open the door to some aspect of ourselves which is hidden away. When our buttons get pushed, it is important not to look at who is pushing them, but what effect this has on us, and why. This is the soul asking us to take responsibility for what happens to us as it leads us back to our relationship with the Divine. Can we relate to another without fear of being overwhelmed, or without needing to possess them? Do we need to get love and nurturing from someone else, because we did not get it from our mothers? Do we find partners who are like our absent fathers in our search to find balance?

Creativity does not mean painting like Leonardo do Vinci. It means allowing yourself to do things for the joy of it; not for money, to fill in time or because you "ought" to do.

THE SOLAR PLEXUS CHAKRA

POSITION: Solar plexus

COLOR: Yellow

DEVELOPMENTAL AGE: 8–12 years old (approximately)

SENSE: Sight

ELEMENT: Fire

CONCERNS: Self worth, determination, identity, personal power, passion

OUT OF BALANCE: Self-centered, no sense of identity, powerless. Need to control, rage. A need to caretake people

BODY SYMPTOMS: Diabetes, liver disease, ulcers, problems with stomach, spleen, and small intestine

SOUL ISSUE: To experience a sense of self worth, self-empowerment, and purpose

The Solar Plexus chakra expresses our sense of power and energy, like an inner sun.

This center is sometimes referred to as the "emotional mind." It is where we experience gut reactions to people and events. It is our power center and where we experience most of our feeling. It is where we give out and take in energy from others. We form strong invisible bondings to others through this chakra and because it is a power center, we need to understand that the energy here is not for use over others, but for our own sense of self empowerment. It is concerned with our sense of who we are as a soul-directed human being.

The solar plexus and identity

The Base chakra is about our relationship to the world and our will to survive, whereas the Sacral chakra is about our relationship to others and our will to create. The Solar Plexus chakra is about our sense of who we are in the world and our will to be.

Around the age of eight years old this center begins to develop. At that age, a child knows that it is here, there are others here as well, so now it is time to begin developing a sense of self—or "who I am." The ego begins to develop and this can start to produce problems. There is a need for self-expression and independence, and it is a difficult time for parents who try to find the balance between allowing the right degree of freedom combined with protection which prevents inexperience leading to disaster. If your parents and teachers do all the choosing for you during this phase of development you may become a rebel, or take on the shape that those around you are trying to mold you into. The upper age of the Solar Plexus chakra marks the onset of puberty, which is another major time of change. At this age it is important to develop ego and personality as these take us out into the world. If we do not develop a sense of who we are, we remain victims or caretakers of others. Or we need other people to tell us who we are, because we do not know ourselves. Later this center will need to relinquish its position as captain of the ship and hand over to guidance from the level of the soul—often a difficult transition—but at the age of 8 to 12, we are not yet concerned with these things. The challenge of the Solar Plexus chakra is not to fall into the polarities of bully or victim, master or slave but to find a balance. We need to establish who on earth we are before we realize who we are in Heaven's name.

This center is called the emotional mind because what we think has a great effect on our feelings. A thought about something that irritates you, if given space, can develop into a full-blown rage. Rage has a huge energy that can make people feel powerful and in control of others; yet underneath it is a person who feels small and vulnerable. Or, if you feel "less" than others you will find yourself doing anything for a quiet life—at the expense of your own wishes.

The Solar Plexus is where we get butterflies in the stomach and "gut reactions." Emotional or mental stress affects the functioning of this chakra, which can result in the body expressing its disease with ulcers, digestive disorders, or comfort eating. Reflect on the questions overleaf which relate to this power-house of yours.

Questions for the Plexus chakra

Think about these questions and write your responses in your journal:

Do you give away your power to please others? and then feel guilty or resentful?

✳

Do you have a temper and an inability to listen to another's point of view?

✳

Are you aware of your emotions? How do you respond to them?

✳

Can you express your emotions in a calm and honest way?

✳

Who annoys you? Does this reflect something back to you about yourself?

✳

Are you afraid to say no?

The Solar Plexus is the center that needs the most protection, you need to be aware of what is happening there. One way to do this is to close your eyes and focus your attention on that area of your body. Concentrate on your breathing, breathing out any tension or anxiety you may be feeling there, and then imagine that center to be like a flower, gently closing.

Now in your mind's eye imagine a disc in front of that area that is marked with equal armed cross. that will protect you from "giving out" or "giving in" inappropriately.

Now say to yourself:
"I am in control of my own power. I am able to make my own decision."

THE HEART CHAKRA

POSITION: Center of chest

COLOR: Green with Rose Pink

DEVELOPMENTAL AGE: 12–15 years old

ENDOCRINE GLAND: Thymus

SENSE: Touch

ELEMENT: Air

CONCERNS: Compassion, love without conditions, vulnerability, tenderness, detachment, hurt, bitterness, courage, forgiveness

OUT OF BALANCE: Inability to give or receive love, expectations of others, inability to love (or, at least, accept) yourself

BODY SYMPTOM: Heart and vascular disease, diseases of the immune system (allergies, cancer, AIDS, ME)

SOUL ISSUE: To give and receive love without condition, to find strength in vulnerability, to listen to your heart, the seat of your soul

The Heart chakra expresses the state of love in your life – both unconditional and egotistic.

The Heart chakra needs more focus than the others in contemporary times. We are making the shift from the Age of Pisces to Aquarius, represented in the chakra system by the move from the solar plexus to the heart. In other words taking our focus from personal power to open-hearted, inter-dependency. Moving from the love of power to the power of love.

Love? In Sanskrit (an ancient Indian language) there are over 60 different words to describe the different faces of love. In the West we have only one that we use to describe our feelings about everything from hot buttered toast to God. The love that is the true feeling of the Heart chakra is called unconditional love, which means that it is freely given without any expectation of getting something in return. But first we need to look inside and until we can begin to love ourselves, we can never truly love another. "Love they neighbor as thyself," said Jesus. We remember the part about loving our neighbors, but somehow the last two words escape our attention. Perhaps that is because loving yourself conjures up images of preening in front of mirrors and strutting around saying "I am the greatest." Those postures belong to the ego and personality—they are not the attributes of true Heart love.

Perhaps we do not understand the meaning of this unconditional love because we have never experienced it. Love was shown to us when we behaved in a certain way, or if we ate up our lunch or maybe stopped crying.

There are many people who have demonstrated the true love of the heart: the late Mother Teresa who worked in appaling conditions with the poor and sick in India and wanted nothing for herself in return; Nelson

His Holiness the Dalai Lama

Mandela, the South African president, who holds no bitterness from his long sojourn in prison, and the Dalai Lama who is a serene ambassador for Buddhism, despite the fact that his country (Tibet) and culture have been ruined by China.

Just think for a moment of the many ways we refer to our hearts, and when we say these things we are not thinking about a mechanical pump that moves blood around our bodies:

Questions for the Heart

Think of someone you have loved. How would you describe the quality
of your love for them?

✳

How does it feel? Experience the feelings which come with that image.

✳

What do you expect from them?

✳

Are you able to tell someone you love them without being certain of their response?

✳

Bring up an image of someone you do not like, can you see with your heart what
it is they are here to teach you?

✳

Is there someone, or some situation you would like to forgive and release?

✳

What are your feelings about your Self? Are they judgements?

✳

What makes your heart sing?

✳

Take time to really think about each question, and write your responses,
from the heart, in your journal.

✳ Broken-hearted
✳ Home is where the heart is
✳ Getting to the heart of it
✳ Heart-felt feelings
✳ Harden your heart
✳ Heart and soul
✳ Big-hearted
✳ Warm-hearted
✳ Open-hearted
✳ Heart to heart

What are the qualities that we are referring to when we use the word "heart" in this way? They are a different set of feelings from the ones that go on in the solar plexus, aren't they? Mercy, compassion, tenderness, peace, joy, true love, sister and brotherhood—these are not feelings that are conditioned by the mind, they come from the very heart of us. One of the most important aspect of Heart love is that it is non-judgmental. We have become adept at making judgements about ourselves and other people. While there is judgement, there is no Heart love. We have no idea what goes on in another person's skin. We have no idea what lessons they have come here to learn or how early life experience has shaped a bully, rapist or murderer. That does not mean their behaviour has to be condoned, but that it is treated with the understanding that we are all part of the same whole, and that whole includes a dark side as well as a good side. The heart understands this because it is the interface between Heaven and Earth. It is the chakra in the middle of the chakra system. The three lower chakras (the Base, Sacral, and Solar Plexus) are concerned with life on Earth, while the three higher centers with their higher frequencies are more in touch with the realms above the physical plane.

The heart is the meeting ground for Heaven and Earth. Going back to the roots of religious belief we find the heart representing the soul. The ancient Egyptians believed that after death it was weighed against the feather of Truth. If your heart was found to be heavy and cluttered with attachments to physical existence, then you needed to have another go, to experience another lifetime until the heart was filled with light. The winged heart is the symbol used by the Muslim Sufi order, and it was also used by Jesus as a symbol of his teachings.

What stops us from opening our hearts to ourselves and others? Fear: fear of exposing our vulnerabilities, of being taken advantage of, of losing power, or appearing too soft? These, once again, are messages from the ego and Solar Plexus that do not understand that there is a strength to be found in admitting

our weaknesses. We are all wounded in some way, after all. Heart love is not like money—give it all away and then there is a bankruptcy situation. With love, the more you give, without expectation of receiving, the more you receive.

Our arms and hands are closely linked to our hearts. We talk about "being touched" by his kindness, or "reaching out" to give support. The arms and hands are an extension of the heart and we can express our heart-felt feelings towards another with just a gentle touch. We use our arms to hug and embrace, bringing ourselves together, heart-to-heart.

The heart under siege

When this center is out of balance, our bodies express their disease with cardiovascular problems (losing heart, hardening of the heart), diseases of the immune system which include HIV, cancer and ME (feeling fearful and unprotected) and allergies and hypersensitivity (feeling the need to be acutely sensitive at all times, being afraid once more).

Giving your self some time—to relax, meditate, or just sit—allows your system to move out of busy mode. Your body, mind, and soul gets the message that you value yourself enough to disengage from the frantic whirl of daily life to pay attention to your own personal needs. That is loving yourself. Don't just do something, sit there! And while you are just sitting there, concentrate on your breathing to focus on your Heart chakra.

Then make the following affirmation: "I feel compassion for myself and all living beings."

THE THROAT CHAKRA

POSITION: Throat

COLOR: Turquoise/Aquamarine

DEVELOPMENTAL AGE: 15–21 years old

SENSE: Hearing

ENDOCRINE GLAND: Thyroid

ELEMENT: Ether

CONCERNS: Self-expression, trust, freedom.

OUT OF BALANCE: Incessant chattering, feeling "choked." Inability to speak up and speak out

BODY SYMPTOM: Problems of the thyroid, sore throat, tonsillitis, hearing difficulties, tinnitus

SOUL ISSUE: To feel free to speak honestly and openly. To trust the soul to speak its truth

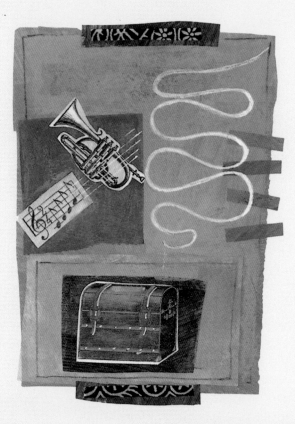

Speech and self-expression are the values of the Throat chakra—do you speak you mind or lock up your thoughts?

Questions for the Throat

If I say what I think, will people still like me?

✳

If I speak my mind, will I be understood?

✳

If I let people know who I really am, will I be accepted?

✳

If I say what I want, will people think I'm selfish?

✳

If I say what I feel, will I hurt other people?
Does that stop me from speaking up and speaking out?

"In the beginning was the Word and the Word was with God and the Word was God." These are the opening verses of St John's gospel. Every word has a sound; in fact, everything has its own "note."

Some scientists are beginning to believe that sound created the pattern that enabled the Universe to come into being. Sound is vibration, an invisible energy, which creates form. Everything then, was created from a certain sound which created that particular form.

Every individual has a unique fingerprint, DNA structure and also their own unique sound or note. The throat center is concerned with the expression of that note and how it is communicated. It also has a direct link with the second chakra, the sacral center, which deals with relationships. The Sacral chakra is about the relationships we have with other on the physical plane—the Throat chakra is about a different relationship: the relationship that exists between our personality/ego self and our soul. Honest communication is speaking with a voice that is not dictated to by the poor ego who needs to have its existence confirmed, and will go to any lengths to achieve this end. If you are an inflated bag of nothing, which is what the ego becomes, you, too, might need to have your existence validated! The soul, however, simply needs to express its truth. This center gets out of balance when the ego or personality insists on voicing its own plans and beliefs in preference to listening to, and expressing, those statements that come from the soul.

This chakra is also linked to our hearing. Our ears allow us to hear what we are saying and to check, at a deeper level, whether what we express is true to the impulse of the soul. If there are problems with your hearing, is there something, an inner voice is telling you, that you are choosing not to listen to? It is not always easy to speak up and speak out, but honest communication always has a positive outcome. It's not what you say, but the way that you say it. Blurting things out, or shouting at someone will probably not have the desired effect. There is always another way to say it, and if the statement comes from the heart, it will be heard at that level too. The other side of this coin is to always keep quiet. Sometimes it can feel safer to do that, but it ends in repressed, depressed feelings and a sense of being "choked" by life.

Toning and chanting (as religious sects have known for centuries) affect the whole vibration of our being. Like an auric workout, they clear the airwaves and allow us to tune into our Throat chakra and our own individual note.

Try this:

Close your eyes and bring up an image of a situation where you want to say something, but have not as yet been able to.

Now imagine yourself saying what it is you want to say in this situation. Is this what you really want to say? Or do you need to say something else that lies behind this?

Now just close your eyes and make this affirmation:

"I express my deepest thoughts and feelings with clarity."

THE BROW CHAKRA OR THIRD EYE

POSITION: Above and between the eyes

COLOR: Indigo blue

ENDOCRINE GLAND: Pituitary

SENSE: None

ELEMENTS: None

CONCERNS: Intuition, inspiration, confusion, clarity

Out of balance: Lack of trust in intuition, inability to let go of logic, always in "another world," nightmares

BODY SYMPTOM: Tension headaches, migraine, visual problems, sinusitis

SOUL ISSUE: To trust the insight and intuition that comes from the perspective of your soul. To "see" beyond everyday limitations

As the pituitary gland is the conductor of the endocrine orchestra, so the Brow chakra is the command center of the chakra system. Here resides the managing director or overseer. It is the balance point between the left and right functions of the brain. From this point it is possible to "see" in all directions. It looks out into the world, it sees what the soul needs to observe and it has an overview of the whole chakra system. Note how many references have been made to functions associated with our physical eyes. This chakra is concerned with "seeing" of a very different nature—insight, inner vision and intuition—how we really "see" things. Often our insights are ignored because our gut reactions, based on the needs of our personality, shout louder. Your intuition speaks only to you. The gut reactions are based on

The Brow chakra is concerned with our inner vision—insight that helps us see beyond the surface of life to the deeper, more soul-ful levels.

previous experiences and may lead you down the wrong path or keep you tied to a treadmill.

When we live life purely at the level of personality or ego, we struggle with the issues of insecurity, lack of confidence, the need to be needed, feelings of being unloved, loss of control and other problems that are the concerns of the ego. To redress this balance, we need to realize that the vision of the soul is being ignored, and a compromise must be reached. The overseer needs to hear the work force but not to let that work force run the company. The conductor of the orchestra knows the importance of hearing all the instruments to produce harmony.

As we begin to realize that there is more to us than we thought there was, our consciousness expands. As this expands, we discover new ways of using our minds. The activation of this chakra increases our powers of visualization, or seeing with the mind's eye. This picture-making ability has the power to evoke not only the image itself, but a whole range of emotions and feelings. These abilities are the domain of the right hemisphere of the brain, which is also responsible for symbolic representations of the world. For example, dreams speak to us through symbols, and in this way they bring messages to our conscious mind about matters that need some attention. Colloquially, we speak about being in our "right mind." Scientists, doctors, and psychiatrists now take seriously the right mind (brain), seeing it as a valuable tool with which to regain our whole psyche.

As speech relates to the Throat chakra, visual images are connected to the Brow chakra. Try this little experiment—the Brow chakra exercise, below—remembering there is no right or wrong way of doing anything. Just allow it to happen—and know that whatever happens is fine, even if nothing occurs.

This is an affirmation for the Brow chakra: "I trust my insight. I am in tune with an infinite source of guidance."

Exercise for the Brow or Third eye chakra

Think and feel now of a situation that is concerning you. How do your feel you would like the outcome to be? Now take your awareness to your Brow center, just breathing into it, and imagining it opening like a flower, a flower that is the color of the night sky. Now from that place of inner awareness and transcendent vision, review that situation again. Notice the difference between your two views. Write your experience in your journal—this will help you to anchor it.

THE CROWN CHAKRA

POSITION: Top of the head

COLOR: Violet/amethyst, silver/gold

ENDOCRINE GLAND: Pineal

SENSE: None

ELEMENT: None

CONCERNS: Connection with the Divine, Knowing the Unknowable.

OUT OF BALANCE: Despair, no sense of connection to a higher power

BODY SYMPTOM: Depression, Parkinson's disease, epilepsy, senile dementia, brain disorders

SOUL ISSUE: To become Self-conscious

The Crown chakra is our connection to the divine, and is the point on our bodies where energy can enter our being.

At a physical level, this chakra is linked to the pineal gland, which is a light detector. The Crown chakra is where the light of the soul is linked with the Will of the Creator, or the Divine. To use a more mundane metaphor, it is through the crown that we communicate with the Upstairs Management. It is important to remember that this has nothing to do with control, it is a source of guidance from the highest level. It is always available, we only have to ask.

Saints and holy people are depicted with a light or halo surrounding their heads—this is the expanded Crown chakra, shining like a beacon, beaming out the fact that the body and soul are one—being in the world, but not actually of it. It is through the Crown chakra that we experience the highest states of meditation, that take us into a state beyond words—an experience of nothingness beyond mind, body and emotions. But to work only with the higher centers without knowledge of the others is like using a power tool that is not "earthed." Making contact with the energies of the Brow and Crown chakras unblocks the channels which enable the personality to receive light, strength and joy from the Divine source. When the power of the soul and spirit flows in, then no task has to be undertaken using the limited strength of the little ego alone, and surrender does not feel like a threat.

Total despair is demonstrated when someone places their hands over the top of their heads. They feel as if they have lost connection with life itself. Blessings are conferred here and perhaps the pointed hats of bishops and witches are there to act as "lightening" conductors.

The Sanskrit name for this chakra is "Sahasrara," meaning "thousandfold." Another name for this place of connection to the Divine is the "thousand-petalled lotus." The color associated with this chakra is violet or amethyst, so we have now traversed the spectrum of the rainbow from red to violet, from earth to heaven, from matter to spirit. Spiritual awakening is about liberation and the quest for what is really real. It is about experience, not dogma. The thousandfold mysteries of the Crown chakra beckon to us like a lighthouse in the darkness, unfailingly drawing us home.

The affirmation for this chakra is:
"I am that I am."

This is a visualization to help you open and strengthen your chakras. Notice if you have difficulty with any particular chakra, and see if you can understand what that might be about. Our chakras, like our aura, are influenced by internal and external changes in the daily pattern of our lives. Becoming aware of our personal patterns brings understanding that there are those days when we feel low and insecure—we can't be bright and lively 365 days of the year. Doing the Chakra journey, overleaf, will help restore and maintain balance between all the chakras. For this guided meditation sit quietly on a chair (see page 53), remembering to record the words on tape before you begin.

Journey through the chakras

✷ I breathe out any tension in my body and begin to relax knowing that I can use my energy in other, more interesting ways. I imagine my spine is like a stalk, it's as if there is an invisible connection from the base of my spine down into the Earth and this keeps me grounded. The other end of the stalk is aligned to a point of bright light above my head. I take my awareness to my Root chakra, which is at that point between my legs called the perineum. My Root chakra is like a spinning vortex which opens towards the Earth. I breathe into the Root chakra and imagine a vibrant, red flower opening there now, I feel the energy increase in that center. I change my focus to my exhaling breath now, and breathe out any feelings that it's not safe to be here, any feelings of insecurity, I breathe them all out. I say to myself: "I am part of the living Universe. I acknowledge my connection to all living things. I am fully alive and here in my body, I have everything I need."

✳ Now I take my attention to my second chakra, the Sacral or water sexual center, just below my navel, and I breathe in orange, deep orange. And as I breathe color into this chakra it opens like a flower, now I change my focus to my exhaling breath. I breathe out any thoughts about my sexuality that I no longer need. I breathe out any feelings that I am not creative, I breathe out old pictures and memories of relationships held in this chakra that I no longer need—these thoughts and feelings limit me. I breathe them out. Now I say "I have the power to create. I am able to bring something new into this life. I feel confident about my sexuality and my relationship with others."

✳ I take my focus to my Solar Plexus chakra, my power center, and I breathe yellow into this chakra, beautiful solar yellow. As I breathe yellow into my center of personal power, I get a sense of the energy of this chakra as it opens up. Now I change the focus to my exhaling breath and I breathe out any feelings that I have to become perfect. I breathe out any feelings of being a victim or powerless in certain situations, any worries about what anyone else may think, or resentments towards authority. I breathe it all out of my Solar Plexus, and now I say "I am in control of my own power. I am able to make my own decisions. I respect myself and others, I am powerful."

✳ Now I take my attention to my Heart chakra. I breathe in beautiful green to the center of my chest. I become aware of this center of love without condition, expanding and opening up. I breathe this flower open, this is the center where the power of love resides. I breathe in green and feel that power. Now I focus on my exhaling breath, and I breathe out any feelings that I will get hurt, feelings about being vulnerable, about loving others if or when they do something. I breathe out all those beliefs about love that limits and contracts the heart. I breathe out any beliefs that I do not deserve love, that it's wrong to love myself, and then I say "I feel compassion for myself and all living beings: I give and receive love without condition—I am full with love."

✳ I take my awareness to my Throat chakra, and I breathe in a beautiful blue, an aquamarine or turquoise blue. I breathe in this color and get a sense of the flower of my throat chakra expanding. This is my center of honest communication, of speaking up and speaking out freely and openly. I breathe blue into this center. I focus on my exhaling breath, and breathe out any feelings or memories of situations where I was afraid to say what I felt, when I couldn't speak my mind. I say, "I express my deepest thoughts and feelings with clarity: I can speak openly and freely, I trust my soul to speak."

✳ Now I take my awareness to my Third Eye, or Brow chakra, and I breathe indigo blue, a beautiful dark blue, the color of the night sky into this center of inner vision, insight and intuition. I breathe this chakra open, and as it opens up it becomes a gateway for my spiritual awareness. It becomes the eye that sees in all directions, it shows me the way to expand my entire being. I say "I am in tune with an infinite source of guidance. I trust my intuition."

✳ Now I take my consciousness to a point just above my head to the Crown chakra. Here there are the energy colors of white, gold and amethyst. I imagine these colors and breathe them into the space just above my head. This is the place where my halo exists, my knowledge that there is more than a physical reality. As I focus on this chakra, I move into a place of nothingness that is also everything. This is the gateway of the soul, there is nothing to say here, because it is a place beyond words, a placed where I connect my whole being with the Universe. I am the Universe, unlimited and timeless . I hear myself saying "I am that I am."

✳ Now I imagine myself radiating all these colors of the rainbow, all the colors of the spectrum. I see them spin and rotate within me, all the colors that make up white. I am in a shining white light, I become the white light. I allow all the cells and atoms in my body to remember the lightness of being.

✳ Then, when I feel ready, I gently bring my awareness back into the room, knowing that I am connected to Mother Earth and guided by a Divine power, I am centered and focused, I take some deep breaths and gently move my fingers and toes as I open my eyes and come back into everyday reality.

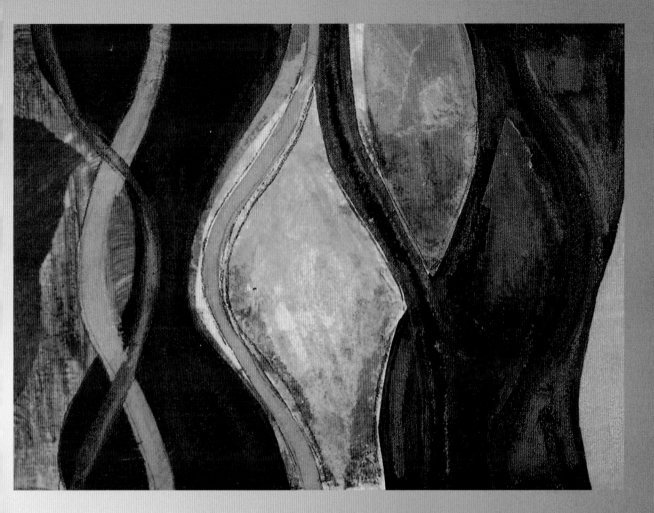

NOTE

Be aware of which chakra you respon from in any situation. Pay attention to both ends (polarities) of the chakra spectrum—connect with Mother Earth as well as Father Sky. Notice what colors you like or dislike; how does that relate to the issues of the chakra of that color? To bring about balance, get some paper, or cloth of that color, and place it somewhere so that you see it each day.

Each color has a different vibration and your subtle anatomy will pick up the frequency from the cloth or paper. Become more aware of your heart energy and use it.

Crystal Power

Crystals act as transmitters and amplifiers of information. Before use, cleanse crystals under clean, cold, running water.

Before crystals became a prerequisite for every new-age traveler, they had already become an invaluable tool in technological advances. As technology makes visible what was previously only seen by clairvoyants and shamans, the invisible becomes visible.

Due to the development of the ruby-powered laser in the 1960s, followed by the silicon chip and liquid crystal displays (LCDs), our knowledge of artificially created crystals has grown; biologists have come to recognize that many of the cellular membranes and structures within our own bodies are liquid crystals as well. It is the ability of a crystal to store, transmit, amplify, and receive information that interests both scientists and the explorer of expanding consciousness alike.

Different crystals work for different purposes. So that you can harness their energetic support, it is important to pay attention to their health and welfare. Crystals have a consciousness, but they do not have a conscience. They may be used to transmit, receive, and amplify specific energy. The quality of that energy depends on the user. Again, like electricity, it is a specific power source that may be used for positive or negative results.

Crystals are neutral in themselves, but they can be charged with whatever energy we put into them. This energy can then be transmitted into the atmosphere, or another person's aura, thoughts, or energy body.

Crystals for personal use

The uses for crystals are endless. You may feel drawn to wearing or holding them for healing or to help keep you in balance; holding a particular crystal during meditation amplifies the effect. You can place crystals around your house because of their beauty. They give off negative ions, which create a sense of wellbeing.

The color of the stone or crystal that you are drawn to is significant, as it relates to that frequency within your aura and chakra system that may require support. In fact, the color relating to the chakra may not be the same the color of the stone; it is the frequency that is important.

Crystals and the chakras

AGATE is used to balance, calm, and stabilize (blue agate); energize (red/fire agate); and to support, and build self-esteem (moss agate).
Chakra healing: Base, Solar Plexus, Throat chakras, according to the color.

AMETHYST is used to support meditation practices, for healing, inducing sleep, calming, and cleansing.
Chakra healing: Third Eye and Crown chakras.

AQUAMARINE aids mental clarity and enhances creativity; it can help to ease stress and fear.
Chakra healing: Throat chakra.

BLOODSTONE aids clairvoyance, helps with blood disorders, and with connecting with the earth.
Chakra healing: Base chakra.

CLEAR QUARTZ CRYSTAL does just about everything. It also amplifies the effects of other crystals.
Chakra healing: Can help all chakras, but specifically the Crown.

CITRINE encourages openness and emotional maturity, helps cope with fear, encourages physical endurance, and mental clarity.
Chakra healing: Sacral, Solar Plexus chakra.

HEMATITE is a "grounding" crystal and is used for transforming negativity.
Chakra healing: Base and Throat chakras.

JADE is used to inspire, protect, and vitalize, to encourage harmony and regulate the heart.
Chakra healing: Solar Plexus, Heart chakra.

LAPIS LAZULI is for boosting insight, intuition, and mental clarity.
Chakra healing: Throat and Third Eye chakras.

MALACHITE promotes meditation and dream work. An anti-depressant, this soothing stone gives strength and courage.
Chakra healing: Solar Plexus, Heart chakra.

MOONSTONE is used to balance over-sensitivity and encourage the feminine aspect. Also used for promoting openness and awareness.
Chakra healing: Sacral and Heart chakras.

ROSE QUARTZ encourages unconditional love, and helps release any negativity.
Chakra healing: Base and Solar Plexus chakras, but especially the Heart chakra.

TIGER'S EYE is grounding, and helps with concentration and creativity.
Chakra healing: Base and Sacral chakra.

TURQUOISE protects and aids communication.
Chakra healing: Throat chakra.

CHAPTER 5

Healing

What is healing?

A healer "channels" energy by visualizing it as bright light, colors, or an energy force that travels through the healer to the person recieving the healing. The healer can work remotely, through visualization, amd if present may lay their hands on the person or place their hands close to, but not touching, their body.

What are the benefits of healing?

It is a safe, non-invasive technique used to ease ailments and illness, and to boost energy. The flow of energy from the healer helps re-tune the body, emotions, and spirit, bringing feelings of well-being, vitality and calm.

Can anyone heal?

Yes—you can heal with your hands, and also use sound, crystals, and color.

To heal means to make whole, which does not always mean making someone well and healthy. Illness is there for a reason, and if we can see the learning potential behind this expression of the body's disease, the deeper significance of signs and symptoms will be revealed. It is another way that the soul draws our attention to patterns of behavior that stand between us and our connection to the Divine.

The greatest healer that we know of was Jesus. He said, "All these things you can do and more," which is a pretty encouraging statement if we would only believe it. Unfortunately, the church did not encourage people to think in this way—it was easier to control them if they all thought they were sinners and God was a god of punishment and retribution. As the church established itself as a political institution, "gifts of the spirit" posed a threat to their authority and control, and any attempt to heal was decreed to be the work of the devil (whoever he is). Hence the Witchcraft Act, under which at least eight million "witches" (probably just healers and herbalists) were put to death in the Dark Ages, all in the name of a religion, the leader of which stated "They shall lay hands on the sick and they shall recover." Dark ages indeed.

The Caduceus

The symbol of the medical profession is the caduceus—a staff with two serpents twining round it. This has its origins as far back as ancient Egypt, a highly advanced civilization that understood the laws of the cosmos and mankind's place in it. The snake or serpent was an important symbol for the process of life, death, and transition and perhaps in the form of the caduceus it represents the double-stranded helix of the DNA—the very blueprint of all life forms. A snake sheds its skin when it becomes old and outworn. We would be healthier if we did the same, instead of hanging on to the old skin that covers up fresh, new growth.

Balancing our life force

Health is dependent upon balancing strong to weak, seeking to balance the *chi* or the life force within us. The pressures of life make this difficult and sometimes impossible. Your mind cannot focus, your emotions are all over the place, and your body begins to develop aches and pains. Perhaps you decide to go to see a healer or get yourself on a list for absent healing (see page 96. What exactly happens? Professor Alan Wolf explains this process by saying, "The fundemental proposition is that everything is vibrating, everything is vibration. If you can vibrate with it, or attune whatever it is that is vibrating, a resonance is created; then you have a way of transferring energy back and forth." This is known as the tuning-fork effect. If two people each hold a tuning fork that is pitched to the same note and one tuning fork is sounded the other will vibrate as well, as the resonant energy is transferred between the two.

Energy moves from strong to weak, seeking balance. Everyone has their own self-healing mechanism which works at a level below conscious thought. You do not have to tell your skin to heal when you cut your finger any more than you have to tell your white blood corpuscles to fend off an invading virus. These things happen all by themselves as the body continually seeks equilibrium or homeostasis. Sometimes the balance is disturbed too much and we become ill, or perhaps the body's self-healing mechanism has become a bit run down. A few days "out of life" may well be all that is required, but going to a healer, or asking for absent healing, will assist the body to return to health and balance much more rapidly. The healer is the tuning fork, setting up a certain frequency within themselves, to give your self-healing mechanism an energy boost—rather like using jump leads when your car battery is flat.

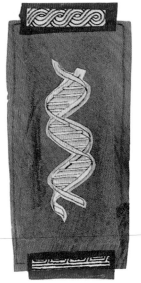

DNA structure

Trees are popular emblems of holistic healing. Particular species, such as the oak, also have their own healing attributes. One of the most famous is found at the ancient Greek sanatorium of Hippocrates, who is regarded as the father of medicine.

Tuning in

The healer will tune in to you and then use himself as a conduit for the life force which will be channelled through him into your energy field. He channels the energy that will give your body chemistry a boost. Since energy flows from strong to weak, he will be bringing up your energy, encouraging it to come back into balance.

Healing is different from curing. It helps to address the cause of disease rather than the effect or symptom. Orthodox, or allopathic, medicine, deals only with symptoms. Of course there is a place for orthodox medicine, but doctors in the past have (on the whole) been more like mechanics than gardeners. We might need a mechanic or a technician to fix a structural problem, but we need a gardener who understands the nature of the garden to help reach the cause. Complementary health practitioners (which include healers) are gardeners. They do not just look at the one part of the garden that seems out of sorts, but consider all the factors that make up the nature of the garden, to find out where the imbalance is. Perhaps the soil is tired, perhaps there is not enough light, perhaps it has been overcultivated and needs a little wildness. Perhaps part of it has died or been cut down and it needs to express sadness. The garden itself knows deep inside what is amiss.

A healer will not tell you what is wrong with you—he may not know, anyway. He will simply give you that charge of loving life force that will find its own way to the area of need. Healing is not about prescriptions and diagnoses, or working out the "Why me?" of illness. It is simply using the life force, as used by Jesus and many others, to make another person whole.

Healers connect with a source of healing energy appropriate to their intuition and beliefs. This may be a general divine, or universal energy or, for example, that of Jesus Christ or Buddha.

Who can be a healer?

Everybody can, to a certain degree. There are those who have been aware of this gift since birth, knowing that a soft word or gentle touch can make people or animals feel better. These people often report heat or feeling a tingling sensation in their hands. The rest of us may simply feel drawn towards the healing professions and then discover, when we get our heads out of the way, that just by being with someone, without judgement and with compassion, can make them feel better. We have created that space where there is a meeting of two energies and one takes strength from the other. This is where it is important to recognize where that energy is coming from. If, as a healer, you are using your own personal source of supply, you can become drained and exhausted and end up needing healing yourself. By learning to open up to a universal source of energy you simply become the conduit, and in

fact feel energized yourself at the end of giving a healing session.

There are different sources of chi, or life force, which are available and limitless in supply. For example, a Buddhist might see the Buddha as his source of supply, and a Christian would see his as being linked to Christ. A shamanic healer might link to the Earth and another use the energy of a particular star to which they feel affiliated. What is important is the connection to a source of power and energy outside yourself. One of the most transformative healing energies is love. Love protects, nourishes, and harmonizes, as written in this Taoist text:

The people of Tao transcend self
Through loving compassion
Find themselves/In a higher sense
Through loving service
They attain fulfilment.
Tao 7

The healing ritual

Before attempting to give healing to anyone else, it is better to be trained, which will ensure that you do no harm and do not deplete your own energy. If you are not trained, then follow these basic guidelines.

Do not plunge your hands into someone else's auric space without clearing and centering yourself first. This is where an understanding of the subtle anatomy (the aura and chakra system—see page 42) is useful. It ensures that you are grounded, or "earthed," and that you are aligned to the highest point of light. This ensures that you get yourself out of the way (the personality/ego will want to make assessments and judgments, and to know whether it is being done in the "right" way). Has it worked? Do they feel better? Can I do harm? All those questions fall away when you do the following:

Relax and cleanse your own space. You can do this by imagining yourself standing under a crystal-clear waterfall. The water enters through the top of your head and comes out through the ends of your toes and fingers, taking with it any slow-frequency negativity. Fill yourself up with this sparkling energy. Center and attune yourself by saying "Thy Will (not mine) be done."

Imagine that you are bringing energy up from Mother Earth through your feet, and energy down through your crown from the point of light. Feel or sense these energies merging at the Heart chakra. Breathe into your Heart chakra, and feel this energy moving from the heart down the arms to your hands. Don't make any judgments, or try to *do* anything, or feel responsible for the results; that is the responsibility of the person receiving the healing. The most important part of healing is the intention, which is why all healing attempts should be prefaced with the invocation "Thy Will (not mine) be done." This ensures that whatever happens is in line with the recipient's soul purpose.

Attunement before healing involves drawing energy from heaven and earth, above and below you, to your Heart chakra.

It is important never to push people to have healing, and you should have their permission before starting. It is more appropriate if they ask, but people often don't like asking others to do things for them. If you feel someone could benefit from healing, you might say, "Could you do with extra energy to help you?" If they say yes, then make a little ritual: wash your hands, ask the recipient to sit or lie comfortably and, if it feels appropriate, light a candle. Go through the process of attunement. Bring up energy from the Earth, light down from the Divine, which meet at the Heart chakra, then breathe out this energy through your arms and hands. Allow your hands to become an extension of your heart; let them do the sensing of what to do and where to go.

Painful areas

Sometimes it may feel right to place your hands on the area of pain or discomfort, but always ask your patient before touching them. At other times it may feel appropriate to work in the different levels of the auric field or with the individual chakras. Sometimes, just "stroking" the aura of someone in distress can bring peace and relaxation. A healing session can take from five minutes to half an hour. Listen with your hands and sense the energy coming through you—when you feel "that's enough," it's time to stop.

As it is important to attune and open up, so it is equally important to close down when you have finished. If you have been giving hands-on healing, then you must step back from the person to disengage your auric fields and then wash your hands and wrists

under cold, running water to dispel any negative charge.

Opening up and closing down are essential when working with subtle energies. Not closing down means leaving your energy field wide open to external negativity, which can deplete you. The procedure of opening and closing does not have to be labored. Once you have practiced this a few times, it can be done in a matter of minutes. However, it always needs to be done.

Hand-energizing exercise

Sit comfortably in an upright chair, or cross-legged on a cushion if you prefer. Your back should be straight and your hands resting on your thighs with your palms facing upward.

Close your eyes and for a few moments concentrate only on your breathing. Feeling calm and relaxed, focus your attention on the center of your palms. Imagine a light beaming down into those palms. As you breathe in, breathe in light to your palms, breathe it in. The light is absorbed as you breathe in, notice any sensations in your palms now. As you exhale, now project that light out through your hands toward anyone you think needs help at this time.

Here are some other methods of healing, besides the hands-on-variety.

Absent or distant healing

This method uses the same principles of preparation as discussed, except that the person, animal or situation is held in the mind's eye and then the healing energy is projected to them. Like dialling their telephone number, your mind will then link with them and your focus becomes a conduit. Perhaps you can imagine or sense that they are sitting in front of you. You do not have to visualize them in great detail for the healing to work. It has also been proved that directing energy to the whole person rather than specific, localized areas is more effective. But remember that energy always follows thought; simply surrounding that person with the energy of peace and love is enough. Again we do not know what is "right" for that particular person—perhaps they just need support and healing.

Color healing

Sound and color have energy vibrations. In fact, color psychologists have discovered that people

Each of the seven chakra colors has a healing attribute. Healers visualize and project appropriate colors into the aura of the recipient to aid healing.

work better in rooms of certain colors because of how they relate to them. It has been found that new-born babies become ill if they are consistently surrounded by red because it is a stimulating color. Just imagine how we would feel if everything in nature was red instead of green. The vibration of a color affects our subtle body anatomy, and can therefore be used to heal. Of course each color can be used to charge the chakra that relates to that color. Here is a brief guide of how the colors can be used:

RED
Stimulating color, good for warming cold areas, good for energizing circulation, helping to ground people with their heads in the clouds.

ORANGE
Helps to increasing sexual potency, and boosting the immune system.
YELLOW: Can clear a foggy head, can release deep-rooted problems and increase sense of self-worth.

GREEN
Soothes inflammation, helps to balance the Heart chakra, good for general healing, growth and re-generation.

BLUE
Cooling, calming, good for tension and insomnia. Relieves throat problems.

PURPLE AND INDIGO
Help to open the Third Eye chakra and broaden the mind. These colors can relieve fears and inhibitions.

WHITE
symbolizing purity, it contains the whole color spectrum. It is good for energizing and bringing peace and comfort.

To use color when you are helping someone heal, hold the color in your mind and project it into their energy field after you have completed the ritual of attunement (see page 102).

Sound healing

The medical profession already uses ultra-sound as a tool to bring about healing and here there have been many new and exciting discoveries. The whole notion of sound to restore body harmony is becoming more well known. It has been discovered that certain musical frequencies have powerful beneficial effects on a range of problems, from autism to speech impediments. We all know the effects that a piece of music that we like (or dislike) has on us; healing with sound just utilizes this effect in a more focused way.

There is a true story to illustrate this. The abbot of a monastery decided to ban plainsong and chanting; the monk could be employed

more usefully in the gardens or kitchens. No one could understand why, but after a few months, the monks all became ill—not with any critical diseases, but a general malaise. An enlightened visitor to the abbey recognized the connection between the absence of chanting and the poor health of the monks, and persuaded the Abbot to re-install the daily singing of prayer. Within a week the monks recovered their good health.

Simple healing techniques

There are many other ways to offer healing. Being with someone while they offload their problems is a healing action (but remember, you don't have to take their troubles away with you). Paying attention and using your voice as a healing tool may be just what they need.

Sometimes just a touch on the shoulder is a reassurance to someone that they are not alone and will make all the difference to a person feeling down. A random act of kindness not only benefits others, but helps change the collective consciousness (see page 102).

If there is an area of your body that is showing signs of stress, help will be provided by other parts of the body until it regains its balance. If you do not pay attention to the part of your body that is experiencing discomfort, then the whole system can begin to show signs of disease. Getting to the root cause of this distress will prevent its reoccurence. A visit to a professional healer may help to alleviate the symptoms that you are experiencing, but also consider what your body is trying to say. For example, what (or who) is this pain in the neck about? What's happening to my (inner) vision?

Soul focus:

Healing ourselves and others of our inner and outer wounds brings us closer to the experience of soulfulness.

The next meditation guides you through the attunement to healing energy and reminds you how to become a channel for the energy that brings balance and harmony. Remember that the intention is not to "make things better," it is simply to transmit a quality of energy that sets up a resonance, like the tuning fork, where you become the conduit for the frequency of Love.

As before, sit in a comfortable chair with a straight spine, feeling it as the central axis of your being, with you head and neck relaxed, as if you are hanging from an invisible thread. Place your feet firmly on the floor, with your hands resting gently on our knees with the palms facing upward.

There is no great mystique about healing. It is simply a wonderful way to help each another regain balance. None of us is perfect, or we would not be here. Stepping outside our defended boundaries leads to heart-warming expansion—and feeds the soul.

Healing tune-up

✳ I let the tension drain from my body as I take some deep easy breaths.
I feel the tension draining from my shoulders, my chest, my solar plexus
and abdomen, from my hips and thighs right down through my legs and
out through my feet and toes.

✳ As I breathe, I get a sense of the beating of my heart, I get a sense of
my own rhythm. I imagine that this beating is in time with the pulse of
the Universe.

✳ Now I take my awareness down to my feet. Using my exhaling breath,
it is as if I can push invisible roots from the soles of my feet down into
the Earth. I breathe my roots deep down into Mother Earth. Now I use my
inhaling breath to breathe energy up through my roots into my feet, into
my legs and up my thighs until it connects with my red Root chakra. Then
I feel the energy moving up to connect with my orange Sacral chakra, and
then to the powerful yellow of the Solar Plexus chakra. It continues to
move until it reaches the beautiful green of the Heart chakra.

✳ Now I take my focus to a point of Light above my head, a sphere of light
that is just above my head, the Light that connects me to the One true Light.
I feel or imagine that this Light is coming down through the violet Crown
chakra and is connecting with my Third Eye chakra, a deep indigo blue, the
center of insight and intuition.

✳ I feel or sense it moving to connect now with the aquamarine of my
Throat chakra. It then moves down into my heart, meeting and merging with
the energy of Mother Earth. Heaven and Earth united at the Heart chakra.
I feel or get a sense of those two energies now, as one, in my heart. I breathe
into it, I feel a sense of expansion, expanding all the way down my arms to
my hands, my hands that are the outreach of my heart.

✳ Now I can think of someone who is very dear to me. I project this loving energy towards them, saying "Thy Will Be Done," meaning whatever happens is appropriate according to spiritual Law. I send this Love from my heart out to all those hearts that are broken, that have hardened through pain, to open up to forgiveness, compassion, and joy. I can feel this energy moving through my whole being, expanding my cells, my molecules, my atoms . I feel myself strengthening through the energy of my heart. Then I bring my focus back to everyday reality, knowing that this attunement may be done at any moment when some healing is required.

NOTE

All of us can offer healing in some form or another. Always open up and close down before and after giving healing, and remember to make the silent invocation, "Thy Will (not mine) be done." Use your hands as often as you can to "sense" energy. They will become more sensitized the more you use them. Practice on your plants and animals. Never attempt to make diagnoses or tell anyone what you think might be wrong with them. It's not your energy that you are using, but universal energy.

CHAPTER 6

The Psychic Internet

What is the psychic internet?

A name for energy wavelengths, or our sixth sense.

Benefits?

To be more in tune with our soul, deeper nature, and discern genuine intuition from confusion. It is particularly helpful in making difficult decisions or problem-solving.

How do I start?

You can begin with an automatic writing exercise. By letting your unconscious speak freely, you can become more comfortable with your intuition, and transmit and receive energy as messages.

Everyone at one time or another has what they felt was a "psychic" experience—those times when you are thinking of someone only moments before the phone rings, or a letter drops into the mail box and it is from the very person you have had on your mind. Or perhaps you pick up things about people, maybe you get a sense of their past or a strong feeling of an event that is about to happen. Then there are those hunches that you just know you have to listen to, those intuitions that normally prove to be correct.

Understanding that there is another dimensional reality that stands behind the physical world opens us to the concept that there is a communication highway available beyond the limitations of our five physical senses of seeing with our eyes, hearing, touching, tasting, and smelling.

We are all aware of the huge advances in computer technology and know about the internet, or information super highway, from which we can glean information on every conceivable subject. You can send information to a particular individual, or broadcast your ideas in an instant to millions.

So imagine for a moment that your mind is a computer, a computer that stores all information about you according to what you have experienced and recorded on it to date—your own personal database. By entering a certain code, you can link your personal mind-computer to the "psychic Internet."

The six senses: clockwise, from bottom left: taste, touch, sound, smell, sight, and the sixth sense, seen as the subconsious thought, or intuitive messages to our conscious selves. The sixth sense can be expressed as synchronicity, or coincidence, and through our dreams.

Of course, it is also possible to use your mind-computer for daily activities, but how much more exciting to plug into an interconnecting web that has the potential for linking everyone together, mind to mind—through which you can look forward into the potential future and backward to the past, enabling you to determine the consequences of your actions. Not limited by time or space, the psychic internet can access collective knowledge and the highest levels of wisdom; it has already been referred to as the universal energy field, or collective unconscious mind.

Logging on

There are many advantages and some disadvantages in logging into the real internet, and so it is with connecting to the psychic information highway. You need to be able to access the information you want, so time and practice are required before you start. Like opening the door to a house you have never been into and shouting "Is anybody there?" You need to be clear that you only want to meet people if they have your best interests at heart. If you don't know what you're doing there is also the potential for wires to become crossed, delivering incorrect information. It is also important to remember that the information obtained from this higher level must be used to help us live our daily lives in a more purposeful way. It is not appropriate to be so glued to the screen of this level of consciousness that we become space cadets, addicted to a plane of reality that takes us out of the school of life. There is no value in developing a sixth sense if we do not integrate it with the five we already possess.

Psychic abilities

Historically, psychic awareness is as old as the human race. So-called primitive cultures that lived in harmony with nature used the information highway to communicate across great distances, to forecast the weather and to locate their source of food supply. The shamans, witch doctors, and priests of the tribes used this information highway to read the bones, the signs, or sheep's entrails, to foretell the future and look into the database

Palmistry, tea-leaf reading and other divinatory practices are humanity's attempt to make contact with a psychic internet.

of individuals. In our "civilized" world, reading entrails was not feasible, so people who wanted psychic information consulted tea leaves, crystal balls, and palmists. The principle is the same. There are many currently popular methods of tapping into wisdom from a higher level, including the I Ching, tarot cards, and runes, but their effectiveness is dependent upon the intent and integrity of the user. It is not that these so-called divinatory tools have any hidden powers; it is just that they are just a means for expressing information from a level beyond the physical dimension. Again, the quality of information coming through is dependent upon the user. It is also unlikely that you will receive information that is beyond the experience and intellect of the person whom you are consulting.

In the same way that we can all heal to a greater or lesser degree, we can all make our own contact with higher levels of awareness without having to rely on psychics or tarot card readers. These days there are many people channelling information, which is just another way of saying they have logged into the quantum information highway that connects them to another level of consciousness.

We are talking here about opening up or connecting to another level of energy. This energy may be used for whatever purpose we wish. On the psychic information highway we can choose our connections and access knowledge that can improve the quality of life.

Opening up to new energies

One of the by-products of opening up to the understanding that you are more than you thought you were is an increased sensitivity to all energies. You can liken it to opening doors and windows in a house where they have been closed. Once they are open it is wonderful when the sun is shining and you can see amazing new sights and hear sounds that you never knew were there, but it is important to recognize that the weather is not always good, and you do not always want the doors and windows wide open. Psychically, you need to learn to open and close them consciously so that you are protected and always in control. You do not want to find your house full of people that you have not invited in. You also need to shut out any noise and static that is draining and irrelevant. Protection is important. With the right intention and instruction, psychic development can only bring benefit.

Before going into the various ways that this energy, or information, becomes available for people, it is important to understand that energy flows in two ways. It either flows into us or away from us. In ancient China this was referred to as yin energy or yang energy. You may initially find that you are more comfortable with either one or the other. Healing energy, for example, is yang, which is to say that energy comes through you and flows out from you. Yin is the receptive, passive aspect of the same energy. This means that some people find that they are better transmitters (healers) than they are receivers (psychics). Being aware of the quality of these two energies, and noticing which of them you feel more comfortable with is important. If you find transmitting energy (healing) easier, start practicing using your Third Eye chakra so that you can pick up more information about your patients. (see Chapter 4 on Chakras, pages 42–46) for the exercise and affirmation for this chakra.) If on the other hand you find seeing, or channeling, easier, then it would be helpful to practice using more yang energy so that you can incorporate healing into your work, and it will also help you from being overly sensitive or feeling drained after a session. (The hand-energizing exercise see page 88, Chapter 5, will help you with this.)

Increasing your psychic awareness is like opening doors and windows in a house, which allows new energy, or information, to come in

The four receptive senses —sensation, feeling, thinking, and intuition, are governed respectively by the elements of earth, water, air, and fire.

Accessing the psychic highway

Let us now look at how you might experience receiving information from the psychic or quantum information highway. We know that we have an energy system or subtle anatomy that interfaces with our physical body (see pages 32–35), and it is via this energy system that we both receive and transmit information. The different levels of our being have different vibrations, as we have seen, starting with the densest level of the physical body, and moving out to the finer vibrations. All these different

wave bands are interconnecting. The first four levels, then, are body (sensation), emotions (feeling), mental (thinking), and soul (intuition). These are the four receptive senses and they are governed respectively by the four elements of earth, water, air, and fire.

You can receive information via a number of different routes: through your body, your emotions, your mind, or your spiritual self. Different techniques have been traditionally developed to explore these levels of receptivity, such as pendulum dowsing (page 111). Each aspect may be used independently or collectively to pick up information at a psychic level.

Feeling psychic energy

Our physical bodies respond very quickly to different levels of psychic energy. Remember in Chapter 3 on The Aura, it was mentioned how to feel atmospheres or vibes that are emanating from people or places. Think for a moment about the last time you were angry or upset—where did you sense those feelings in your body? Our bodies also respond to joy and fear, don't they? Healers often report feeling heat or tingling in their hands when they are channelling a lot of energy in certain areas to their clients.

They may also become aware of sensations in their own bodies, which will be directly related to those of their clients. People who do divining and dowsing rely on their bodies to access information. Holding a question in their mind that requires a yes/no response, they use a tool such as a pendulum or dowsing rod to amplify the slight muscle twitches that give them the information they require. This ability is known as clairsentince.

Anybody can learn to use a pendulum, so you may want to try to make one for yourself. You can simply hang a ring, a pendant, or a heavy button from a piece of thick thread or string. Commercially made pendulums, specifically for dowsing, may be made of wood, crystal, brass, or stainless steel, but a home-made one works just as well. You can only get a yes or no response from a pendulum, so it is important that you do not ask a question that cannot be responded to in this way. Do not ask emotionally charged questions such as "Should I emigrate to Australia?", or "Will I marry this woman?" as what you want the outcome to be will influence the answer too much.

However, dowsing can be useful for such things as finding out what foods are not good for you, for example. You may be partial to cheese or chocolate, but your body may not agree. Holding your pendulum over a piece of cheese, clear your mind and ask

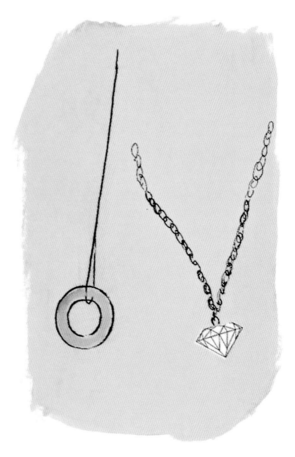

A home-made pendulum, such as a ring on a chain, is as effective as a ready-made pendulum of glass or crystal.

"Is this good for me?". Your pendulum will respond with either "yes" or "no," using the connection between your body-mind and the neuromuscular system.

A pendulum is also useful for finding lost articles. Asking "Are my keys in the house?", "Are they in the bedroom?", and so forth, can help you in your search. For more about this subject it is recommended that you get yourself a book, and then practice (see page 160). However, in the meantime you can find out how your pendulum swings when it is saying "yes" and how it swings when it is saying "no."

Emotional sensitivity to feelings

This response to information being received is best described as gut reaction, and if you are a person that responds easily to the moods of others then it is likely that this faculty is working well within you, and you can develop it as part of your psychic training. It is important to be able to discern between mind-created feelings, or emotions, and those that are coming from deep within. For example, you may be watching a film or listening to a play that evokes a powerful emotional response

Exercise with a pendulum

Make yourself (or buy) a pendulum as described above. The thread should be about 6–10 in (152–250 mm) long. Hold the string or thread between your thumb and first finger, allowing the pendulum to dangle below.

Make sure that your elbow is not stuck to the side of your body. Hold the pendulum over your right knee. Breath evenly and relax. To find out your "yes" and "no" response, ask in your mind the question, "Is this my right knee?" Now wait for a response from the pendulum. Probably the pendulum will begin to move in a clockwise direction (most people's "yes," or positive response) or it may be a forward/backward swinging movement (sometimes this is also "don't know." Let the pendulum tell you what is your response.

To find out what your "no," or negative, response is, hold the pendulum over your left knee this time and ask, "Is this my right knee?" and wait to see what happens. If your positive response is for the pendulum to swing clockwise, your negative response will be for it to swing anticlockwise.

in you. You may find yourself weeping over the plight of children in war zones, or the decimation of rain forests. These are emotional responses to an external stimulus, a stimulus which may touch us deeply and resonate with our own inner feelings of abandonment and sense of grief and outrage at the plundering of our planet, but they are not the feelings that carry information from the psychic level.

Many therapists and counsellors use the feeling aspect of psychic reception with their clients. It enables them to be aware of the fluctuations and nuances in their clients' emotions, and for them to sense what is going on behind the words. When your energy field is open and sensitive, it resonates with the energy fields of places and individuals. It is important to remember that this is not always useful. Picking up other people's feelings can be draining and confusing if you aren't aware of what is going on. It is important to remember that these feelings belong to the other person; do not ever identify with them as your own. Just let them run through you, being aware of how you respond. Don't get emotionally involved, and once again, the need to be centered cannot be over-emphasized. Using the emotional level to receive information is known as psychic empathy.

Thinking – listening with the mind

This has got nothing to do with logical, analytical thought processes of course. We live in times of rational dictatorship. It is interesting to note that although our brain constitutes only 2 per cent of our body weight, it uses 20 per cent of the energy we manufacture, and only 7 per cent of its capabilities. Your mind may be used in two ways in the psychic energy system.

The first involves hearing an inner voice that gives you information. One of the problems that is encountered here is that the logical, left brain will say that what you're hearing is rubbish, or you are "going out of your head". (Perhaps not such a bad thing, after all!) Because there is such a powerful link between language and rational thought mode, it makes it difficult for our intuitive mind to get messages across without being dismissed. For some people, however, inner auditory messages are a very powerful source of insight and wisdom. The ancient Greek philosopher Socrates and the French heroine St Joan of Arc, for example, were guided through their lives by a voice that told them what to do. These messages usually take the form of a voice speaking inside your head, as though it was on a telephone line. This can be in response to a specific question, or sometimes it is information that goes on repeating and repeating itself in your head until you have to pay attention to it. Don't worry - you will not encourage schizophrenic tendencies by utilizing this method of communication - but the most important first step is to become aware of your thinking processes, in other words, to recognize the part of your mind which can independently monitor what another part is doing.

With a little practice, it becomes possible to "hear" yourself thinking about things. As already mentioned, sound is becoming an increasingly important tool in both healing and consciousness-expansion. Of course we need ears to hear, but the ears we need to receive spoken messages from a higher level of consciousness are the inner ears, those ears that are not tuned to the cacophony of sounds our auditory senses are bombarded with from morning till night in our modern world.

Special messages

Another aspect of this inner hearing is automatic writing. In this instance, the information is channeled from a higher course through the arm and pen on to paper.

An example of the value of this method of communication is a book (now in three volumes) called Conversations with God by Neale Donald Walsch, a man in his forties, fed-up with his life on many levels and at the end of his tether. He was in complete despair one day and made the supplication, "If there's anyone there, what on earth is this all about?" To his astonishment, he found himself writing an answer. This was the beginning of an amazing question-and-answer dialogue with an intelligence from another level of consciousness. The clarity, simplicity, and wisdom that emanate from the responses to his questions have the undeniable ring of truth that has made these books into bestsellers.

The wrong messages

There are, however, certain types of messages that you might receive from your internal telephone that you need to be wary of. This applies to all information that you might receive psychically, but especially using this faculty. Watch out for any information that inflates the ego, encourages elitism, intolerance, or induces fear, as this should be disregarded.

Any messages that encourage you or anyone else to believe that they are very special are traps. We are all unique, we all have our own purpose and whether we have been a leader such as Julius Caesar or a gooseherd is neither here nor there in this lifetime. Truly spiritual people don't make a song and dance about themselves. Believing that you have a message to deliver to the world probably won't make catching the No. 49 bus to work any easier. Sometimes this information will come through simply to check whether we have paid attention to the lesson of humility and discernment.

Similarly any messages that encourage intolerance or exclusivity, or that criticise or condemn, need to be ignored. Fundamentalism is on the increase and poses a major threat to civilization. People who believe that their lifestyle or religious belief is the only way of being and believing are subscribing to the old, outworn approach of divide and rule. The age of Aquarius, the age of the Heart, is not about separating one from another. It is about inclusiveness, not exclusiveness. Pay no heed to messages that encourage intolerance of other and inhibit the free will of every soul to make its own choices.

Again, any message that induces fear either in yourself or another also needs to be questioned. You do not need to tell someone that their son is going to have an accident, or that their partner is going to leave them. There is quite enough fear around without creating more. If that happened to be the information that came through, then check the source. We have to take responsibility for what we do with that information. If you pick up a strong sense of impending doom surrounding a person or situation, check the information and dilute it so that it does not invoke panic.

Also be on your guard if there is a quality of fear that underlies a message such as "If you do not believe this, something terrible will happen to you." There is so much fear around nowadays that it is sometimes difficult not to be affected by it, and many people seem to soak up the news peddled by the gloom and doom merchants. Buying into fear, or building on it, increases the psychic pollution surrounding our planet. This is not the way things will change for the better.

There are, however, many benefits from this form of communication, because the answers given are in a form that can be understood—unlike the messages that come through dreams or visual images which speak using symbols and are not always easy to interpret. This particular method of receiving information is known as clairaudience.

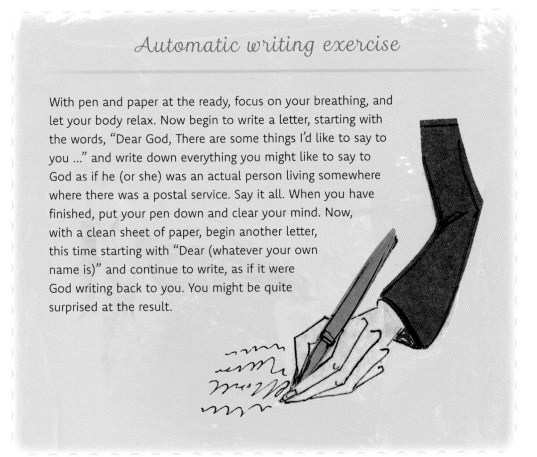

Automatic writing exercise

With pen and paper at the ready, focus on your breathing, and let your body relax. Now begin to write a letter, starting with the words, "Dear God, There are some things I'd like to say to you ..." and write down everything you might like to say to God as if he (or she) was an actual person living somewhere where there was a postal service. Say it all. When you have finished, put your pen down and clear your mind. Now, with a clean sheet of paper, begin another letter, this time starting with "Dear (whatever your own name is)" and continue to write, as if it were God writing back to you. You might be quite surprised at the result.

Intuition, visual imagery, and inner knowing

This mode of communication is closest to the spiritual self. It communicates through visual imagery and inner knowing. The Third Eye, or Brow, chakra is the energy center connected with intuition. We all have an intuitive ability, which can give direction to our lives, connecting us to a higher level of guidance that can be truly life enhancing. As clairaudience is about inner hearing, this faculty is to do with inner seeing—insight, in fact. Some people find it hard to visualize or see imagery, but it does become easier with practice. The Inner Seeing Exercise, opposite, is a simple exercise to determine your visualizing ability:

Inner seeing exercise

Sit comfortably in a chair with your spine erect, your back supported, and your feet placed firmly on the ground. Make sure that your body is relaxed, and your breathing is regular and even.

Close your eyes and imagine that you are standing in front of the entrance to the place where you live and then ask yourself the following questions, visualizing or imagining (not thinking) your reply:

What type of door is it?
What is the color of the door?
What surrounds the door
What type of letterbox does it have?
Where is the bell or door knocker?

When you have answered these questions, go and look at your door to see how accurate your answers were. If you were not able to "see" the door with absolute clarity, it is not an indication that you will be unable to use this method of accessing information. With practice, your imaging ability can be greatly improved.

The important aspect of seeing psychically is being aware of images that come into your mind and being able to interpret them. This Third-eye aspect of your mind relays information in the same way that dreams appear. In dreams, there can be no interference from our conscious ego/personality mind, which will try and block or rationalize such images when we are awake.

How can you believe what you see is true? How do you know it isn't just your imagination? Just your imagination? So strong is the grip of the logical left brain! It was Einstein, no less, who said that "imagination is more important than knowledge". Perhaps it will help the left brain to relax if you tell yourself that you will go along with the images that you see using the magic words "as if they were a dream."

It is important to remember that the language of this faculty is often metaphor or symbol. Seeing the image of a skeleton or coffin does not necessarily mean a physical death, but an ending of some aspect of a person's life. Standing on the edge of a cliff may mean you are about to make a quantum leap for change: doors may indicate openings or closing. Different animals all have their own symbolism in the same way that gardens, houses, trees, and landscapes all have an important significance beyond their literal meaning.

This mode of communication with the psychic information highway is, of course, called clairvoyance—or clear-seeing. Many

Different animals all have their own symbolism in the same way that gardens, houses, trees, and landscapes all have a significance beyond their literal meaning.

clairvoyants can read auras. We know that our subtle anatomy registers the effects of our thoughts and feelings, so anyone who has this ability can literally interpret what they "see."

Clairvoyants or mediums will often refer to their spirit guides or helpers. A shaman's version of this is the power animal whom he meets in "non-ordinary reality" to guide him towards the information he seeks. And now we have an abundance of channelers as well. Many of those who channel information say that this comes from a spiritual energy source. Unfortunately, there is about as much rubbish given out as there is excellent information. Once again we are called upon to use our own internal truth or "Aha!" detector to determine whether this resonates as valid for us personally or whether it comes under the heading of "So what?"

For shamans, a spirit guide can manifest itself as an animal or bird.

Your spirit guide may appear literally as a guardian angel, or you may sense your guide as a presence without form.

The help of spirit guides

In order to receive information from the highest possible source of wisdom, it is helpful to have a guide or teacher on the inner planes who is more familiar with those levels of consciousness than we are. It is important to establish contact with these guides for yourself, and not necessarily rely on other people or channelers to tell you that they see a nun or a Native American Indian who is keeping an eye on you. Guidance may change during the course of our lives as we grow and develop spiritually. Guides may be a more evolved aspect of our soul group or they may be entities who have signed up for service to those on the physical plane. Whoever they are, they are present to support and direct us and may act as a go-between for communication from those who have left the earthly plane to the people they have left behind.

Your guide may take the form of a guardian angel—or perhaps someone more earthy, such as a Tibetan sage. Whatever their guise, they are spiritual energies that clothe themselves in recognizable garb so that we may more easily identify with them. They might even be a higher aspect of our Self. Who or whatever they are, they are recognizable by their emanations of love and compassion, of total non-judgment, integrity, and wisdom. You will feel more centered, more balanced and clearer for having spent conscious time in their company. They act as the interface between our souls and the light of the Divine which may yet be too bright for us to behold.

We have to ask your guide for help, and it may take a few attempts to make contact, but it is certainly there for you. Remember that as soon as you try to do anything you will create tension and block the free flow of energy. When you get a sense of the form your guide will take by using visualization techniques, it is helpful to make a drawing (which does not have to be a masterpiece) or write down a description of the person you see in your journal. Guides come in many shapes and sizes, sometimes appearing as a field of color or energy, so be mindful that the left brain doesn't make judgments about what it "thinks" a guide should look like.

Think about which of the four faculties you feel drawn to explore. Do you pick up information about others through your body? Do you hear things with your "inner" ear, or are you presented with "pictures"? Whichever it is for you personally, the procedure to explore further is the same: moving forward step by step, keeping your intention clear, staying balanced and relaxed will all ensure that the information you receive will not be contaminated by your own personal static and emotional/mental clutter. Keep it simple.

How to stay protected

One more word, and this is about protection. As Judy Hall, author of *The Art of Psychic Protection*, who has been running groups on psychic development for over 20 years, says: "Above all else, psychic protection is about being fully grounded in your body. If you only have a toehold on the Earth, you will never be fully secure."

As we live in an environment that is not only physically contaminated, but also psychically polluted by clouds of negative energy accumulated over the centuries, it makes sense to take some simple precautions. Again, as we put on a raincoat and take an umbrella when going out into the rain, so our subtle body needs some protection from exposure to potentially harmful conditions. These do not have to take the form of elaborate, time-consuming rituals. A simple safety precaution such as visualizing a protective (white) coat around you works well. Remember, energy follows thought.

Carlos Castenada refers to our personal space, both visible and invisible, as a luminous egg of energy. He says that it is important to pay attention to what happens to this egg of ours, as the contents can be leeched away without our being conscious of it happening. We may use our energy wastefully, or it may be drained away without our conscious knowledge, and we are left feeling washed out and depleted. The following techniques can be used for self-protection. Try them for yourself and see if it makes a difference. The most common one is visualizing, or imagining, the psychic bubble—a variation on the Auric egg visualization in Chapter 3 (see page 58).

PSYCHIC BUBBLE Earth yourself by breathing deeply and visualizing "roots." going down deep into the ground. Guide your breath into a comfortable and relaxed rhythm. Imagine and sense that you are surrounded by a transparent, protective bubble or egg, which keeps away negative vibrations. Spend a little time sensing this bubble all around you, extending over your head, under your feet, completely protecting your back, completely surrounding you. Sense that your own vibrations can exit through the membrane of the bubble, and sense that the bubble does not stop the flow of good energies from coming in. Be very relaxed and comfortable in it. Have a clear sense that unpleasant external energies cannot penetrate through the bubble. As William Bloom, author of Psychic Protection, says "This does not have to be a rigid, unchangeable structure, we can customize it." Perhaps one day we might fill this egg of ours with the color blue, and on another day yellow. We may want it close to our skin, rather like a diving suit—or to expand it out. Make it feel right for you for the moment—allow your intuition to work for you.

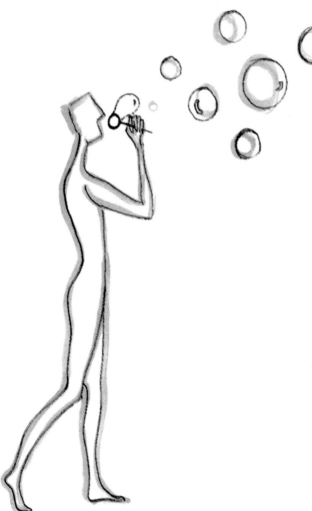

THE FLAME According to William Bloom, this technique is "more dynamic and confident" and may be used in a situation where you need to be active and outgoing, rather than passive—say if you are making a presentation at work, or hosting an event. It suits a positive assertive mood:

Imagine yourself to be a vibrant burning flame. The base of the flame is deep in the Earth, and your body is the core (like a candlewick) of the fire.

You are burning brightly and powerfully. Your dynamism and your glow simply do not allow bad vibrations to get through to you. Bad thoughts and feelings burn up and melt as they come into your radiance. Experiment with different colours; Taught classically, the flame is violet and golden.

Amulets, such as the cross or Egyptian Ankh, help psychic protection.

SHIELDS AND MIRRORS There are many ways to visualize and use psychic shields. Historically the shield was used to protect the physical body from attack. It would often be decorated or painted with talismans or symbols that in themselves were felt to operate on the psychic level, so that both physical and subtle anatomies were being protected.

You can visualize a shield that is big enough to protect your whole body or you can have smaller shields for use on the chakras. For example, you may wish to add some extra protection for the Sacral center (see page 69), if you feel someone is being sexually predatory. Your Solar Plexus chakra may need support if you are in the company of someone who drains your energy or has a spiky emotional field. The simplest and most common form of shield is a circle within which there is an equal armed cross. Other symbol of protection include the Egyptian ankh, the star of David, the caduceus (see page 94) or the calvaric cross.

The mirror is another form of psychic shield. So if you visualize a mirror in front of you it means that any negative energy coming into your psychic field is simple deflected back to its source, creating a boomerang effect.

Perhaps you would prefer to use a different strategy altogether, and that is protection through loving. As psychic Julie Soskin says, "The best form of protection is to become who we really are—beings of love and light. Ultimately your only protection is an open, loving and pure heart."

Loving your enemy is psychologically helpful because it cuts through patterns of victimisation and aggression. It is a statement that you have had enough of unhealthy attitudes and negative vibrations. You just want to get on with a decent life and have positive attitudes. This does not mean adopting a complacent, "you can hit me if you want to" approach to people. It comes from the place of recognition that we are all actors with different roles to play on this stage called life.

Behind every role-player there is an actor who belongs to the same union as you do. Connecting at a soul level helps us hold this perspective, and is an empowering base from which to operate. "Love thine enemy", said Jesus. Take the energy from the Solar Plexus chakra (love of power) up to the Heart chakra (power of love) and see what happens.

The Waterfall cleansing exercise was given in the Chapter 3 on The Aura and Universal Energy Field (see page 32). If you have done it you may already be feeling the effects of it is a powerful visualization for clearing, re-energizing and protecting.

USING PSYCHIC ABILITIES We have all used our psychic abilities in the past, but because orthodox religion took a dim view of people making their own connections to other dimensions, and that included the Divine, we now have to free ourselves from centuries of conditioning that this was an evil or spooky thing to do. For many people, having a spontaneous OBE (out of body experience) or a Near Death Experience has precipitated the opening and development of their psychic abilities. As these happenings increase in number, it makes it easier for us all—the 100th monkey syndrome again (see page 46).

Soul focus:

The right use of psychic energy expands the soul's experience and connects us with other levels of being.

✳

Here is the next guided visualization for you to tape for yourself. This exercise will help you to become familiar with open-ing and closing the Third Eye chakra so that you have control over its use. Before hooking in to the psychic internet, it is essential that you always align yourself to the source of Light, or Divine Will, and imagine that your roots going down deep into Mother Earth. This ensures that you are rooted and guided from a source beyond yourself, which makes it safe to explore. Continue to use your journal to record new insights.

Through the psychic gateway

Sit comfortably in a chair that supports my back, with my feet on the floor and become aware of the central axis of my body. I take some deep easy breaths to relax, breathing out tension and allow my mind to quieten down. Now I say to myself "Thy Will be done." I take my focus down to my feet and imagine that they are growing invisible roots, which I push out into Mother Earth with each exhaling breath.

✳ Now as I breathe in I draw that energy up through my roots and into my feet, up through my legs connecting with my root chakra, breathing it up to my Water/sexual chakra, up to my solar plexus chakra to arrive at my heart.

✳ Now I become aware of a point of Light above my head. This Light is my connection to the Divine, I get a sense of that Light coming down through my Crown chakra and connecting to the indigo blue center of my Third Eye chakra. I feel it expand, and begin to open like a flower. The Light moves down to my Throat chakra, expanding my center of honest communication, and then it goes down to my Heart chakra, connecting with the Earth energy situated there. Heaven and Earth unite at my heart, forming a column of light down the center of my being.

✳ I use my breathing to keep my focus there, and I begin to get a sense of or imagine a door or window in front of my Third Eye. This door or window is closed. Now I imagine that it opens and I can look out through it. Just observing, I close it again. I am in charge of my door or window and can open or close it whenever I want. I open it again and this time I look out, wondering what I might see. I wait for images that may present themselves, perhaps guidance may come for me in some form. There may be a situation where I could use some insight, and look at things from this eagle's perspective to help me see things without interference from my lower, physically-oriented chakras. I just breathe, and wait. Perhaps all I will see will be a beautiful view, or perhaps images will come and go too fast, so I will ask for them to come again. I may hear some words coming into this inner space—just keep feeling relaxed and breathing evenly. I am not trying hard, I'm just holding the focus and waiting.

✳ When I am ready, I bring my focus back through the door or window and close it. Imagine myself having a shower under a crystal clear waterfall—I let the sparkling clarity of this water invigorate and refresh me. I am aware that this water is washing my auric field, taking away any impurities. Now I bring my attention back into my body by taking some deep breaths and moving my fingers and toes. When I am ready, I slowly open my eyes.

NOTE

Be aware of the information that you pick up from others and how that process works. Put your observations down in your journal.In your daily meditations you may like to hold your focus specifically on the Third Eye chakra. Open up the chakras in the usual way (see page 34, the visualization on Opening the chakras), bringing energy up from the Earth and down from your Guiding Light to meet at your Heart chakra. Then take your focus to the Third Eye, breathing into and out from this chakra to encourage its development.

Always remember to "close down" when you have finished (see page 110, the closing down sequence at the end of the Crown chakra exercise).

It is not all right to freely pass on information you may receive about someone unless it is appropriate guidance. Check with them first and be sensitive.

If you become aware of a guide being with you, spend some time to become familiar with them. It is important to ask for the guidance you need.

CHAPTER 7

The Inner Child and Soul

What is an inner child?

This is a part of your nature that can determine how you act in later life.

Why should I know about it?

It can help you understand and resolve patterns of behaviour that may be holding you back. Understanding your inner child, or children, is a fast way to identify your deeper dreams and ambitions in life.

How do I start?

Begin by being absolutely honest about what kind of person you were when you were small—see the profiles on page 127.

If you have ever looked into a baby's eyes, you will have noticed its gaze of frank innocence. There is a total absence of fear, and it is almost as if it is looking right into you. It will hold its observation for as long as it is interested. What is it looking at and taking in?

Our souls require experience on Earth. At this point in our history, they have been here many, many times before, accumulating experience. There will be some outstanding accounts that need to be seen to in order for the books to balance (or we wouldn't be here). It may simply be to experience an uneventful life of peace and prosperity (for a change). It may be that there has been a long, outstanding interaction with another soul, who will be part of your group that needs to be resolved with love and forgiveness. Like a wagon train, we incarnate with the same group over lifetimes, but in each incarnation we will play different roles and switch genders. Perhaps there is unfinished business concerned with passion or power, isolation or illness, betrayal or bereavement. There are as many possible scenarios as there are experiences.

Reincarnation and the existence of karma is a principal belief in Buddhism.

Karmic influences

The people we find closest to us in this lifetime are the ones that we need to connect with again in order to resolve incomplete dramas from before. This unfinished business is called karma (and will be discussed in more detail in Chapter 8 on Reincarnation). Karma is the law of Cause and Effect. Every action has a subsequent reaction. The more powerful the action, the more dramatic the response. Like a pendulum that swings violently in one direction, then the opposite, until after however many swings it takes, it returns to the point of balance in the center—that experience is then complete.

Your soul records all its experiences, but does not judge them as "good" or "bad"—it is all just experience. In order to fully understand the feeling of freedom, you need to have experienced being imprisoned—whether that is literally in jail, or a relationship that imprisons

you. To fully experience a lifetime enriched with love, you need to have felt the pain and sense of separation that lovelessness leads you to. Knowing what it is like to be both with and without takes you to a point of balance. The Way of Non-attachment is how the Buddhists refer to this state. Whatever happens, it is fine, because that is what is needed by the soul.

This perspective takes you away from feeling a victim of fate and circumstance to the understanding that everything, and everyone, has a purpose and meaning to your life.

Before coming down to be part of the "wagon train" again the soul reflects on what experiences are required during this incarnation. It asks: "what sort of parents do I need to help me with that experience" (remember, no judgment about it being good or bad!)? "In what sort of conditions do I need to find myself in, in order to learn?".

Soul contracts

There will be guidance and loving support from Light Beings and others in the soul group, and "contracts" will be drawn up between souls for joint experience. Perhaps the soul of your father or mother contracts to play the difficult role of villain of the piece in order for you to come to a point of forgiveness and understanding that sets you both free. Perhaps another soul commits to a short incarnation and leaves its physical body early, giving others the opportunity of coming to terms with the grief and loss of a child—giving them the chance to turn this pain into something positive. Who knows? The soul certainly does. Which brings us back to the importance of the inner, or Divine Child.

The soul may not fully engage with the body it is going to inhabit until up to a couple of days after birth. Remember from the section on chakras (see pages 40—48) that only the Crown and Base are open at birth to make the connection between Heaven (or Home) and Earth. As the foetus grow into a baby, and is

"Metaphorically, the child carries in its heart a suitcase for its life, packed by its mother." Tian Dayton Ph.D, The Quiet Voice of Soul.

still very much in contact with Home, so the soul's commitment to this little body grows with it. It will begin to pick up the feelings that are going on within the mother that is housing it. And it will become increasingly aware also of her moods and interactions with others.

The soul has just come from a place of unconditional Love, a place of beauty and fine vibration, a place of unity and peace. It is much harder for a soul to arrive into a gross, divided and often hostile world than it is to leave at death and go Home. Imagine the effects on a new-born baby's soul of the more interventionist methods of childbirth— arc lights, peering faces, metal instruments, and being turned upside-down and slapped on the back to make it take its first breath. It is enough to make anyone think twice about whether this was a safe place to be! Natural methods are thankfully making a comeback— midwives and mothers may now have more involvement, and women can choose to deliver in a squatting position rather than having their legs in stirrups. Water births, listening to specially chosen music, and giving birth in the secure environs of home are ultimately more welcoming to the new soul of the baby.

The inner soul child

The new born, innocent and vulnerable soul-child is totally dependent on others for its survival. Physical survival, while obviously fundamental is secondary to the importance of nurture and love. Through love, it retains its sense of "connection." It has just come from a place where Love is the force that holds everything together. The expression of anything other than love from its earthly parents is taken in as being due to some fault of its own. Dr Alexander Lowen, a pioneer in the field of body-oriented psychotherapy, maintains that the feelings of guilt and unworthiness implanted in the first three years of life are almost universal.

Here then is the fundamental wound we all struggle with: separation and a sense of being disconnected. A baby continually looks into its mother's eyes (the windows of the soul) for that connection. Much later on in life we may find ourselves looking for this through music or in nature, or through sex, drugs, and alcohol— in fact, anything that takes away the pain of isolation and loneliness.

Our source of connection is closer to us than anything "out there." It is our own inner, Divine Child—the one who was with you at birth, who remembers her or his place of origin. The one who looked wide-eyed and wondering at the world and who was fascinated by all that there was around her—who became absorbed in watching a beetle, rain on a window pane, daubing mud or splashing in a puddle. Like an open hand, a soft ball of wax—she was ready to receive experience on Earth.

From the beginning, mostly, the world becomes frightening because we have little to do with the shaping of our ball of wax. We sense what is going on around us through our static-free little auric field.

Let's say we experience a trauma of some kind, something that makes us feel unsafe. It might be hearing our parents argue or being left unattended in our cot The open, vulnerable, trusting and innocent Divine Soul-Child splits off and goes somewhere safer, or maybe disappears within. We begin to use coping strategies in our attempts to regain our sense of connection and to feel more secure, but the Divine Child may remain on the ceiling, on top of the wardrobe or where it safe to observe, because being at home in the body is scary.

Stop for a moment and think. In threatening situations in your life today, do you "split off", or go deep within? Below and on the following pages (pages 126–130) are some of the ways that a little person, with no rational means of communicating, might have developed behavioral patterns to support itself. Notice those inner children with which you identify.

THE PLEASER

I suppress my own feelings so that I make everybody else feel all right. If everyone else feels okay they will not reject me. If I please people, they will like me.

Later in life: I don't value myself. I will do anything for a quiet life and often feel guilty. I can only relax when everyone else has everything they want.

THE ACHIEVER

I have to try harder and harder to prove to my parents that I am good enough to be loved. I keep hearing a voice saying: "You could have done better".

Later in life: I am often a workaholic and overstressed. Success is a matter of life or death for me. If I'm not perfect, I will have failed (and I won't be loved).

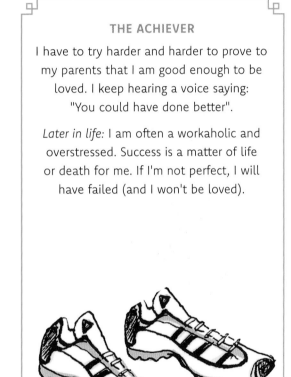

THE REBEL

Pleasing people didn't get me love. My parents were aloof and controlling. The only way I get attention is by making a fuss, or doing something naughty. This meant trouble, but at least they gave me some attention.

Later in life: I like to shock, and I often get angry. It's usually when I feel I am not getting any attention, or people won't do what I want them to do.

THE IDLE DRONE

It seems that nothing I do gets any attention, so I might as well give up—there's no point in trying because whatever I do, they don't love me. I need huge amounts of encouragement to give me confidence.

Later in life: I give up very easily, and often feel bored and lazy.

THE VICTIM

O dear! Nobody loves me! I get attention when I cry and tell Mummy that someone has hurt me or I don't feel well. If I cry enough, I'll think that I will get some love.

Later in life: It's all the fault of the government, or is it everyone around me? Or perhaps it was my mum—or the weather. I can't take any responsibility for my own life, because if I do, then no one will look after me. O yes—it's always someone else's fault that things don't go right in my life.

THE RESCUER

When I was very small I learned that doing things to please my mum or dad made them give me love. The other children the same age as me used to call me a "goody goody" and "teacher's pet" when I went to school.

Later in life: I like victims because I can look after their problems and it means that I don't have to pay attention to any of my own. I'm different from a Pleaser because I rescue people to make sure that they become dependent upn me. This makes me feel in control and needed, and then I feel safe.

Rescuers use other people's problems as escapism, and to make them feel safe and needed.

THE RATIONALIZER

I live in my head, because it's the safest place to be. There was too much emotion around in the family and it nearly frightened me to death—it was so overwhelming. It's much safer to cut out those frightening things called feelings. Or I might have come from a family where feelings weren't acknowledged. I was always told I shouldn't cry or get cross, so I don't really know much about feelings now.

Later in life: Feelings? Don't go in for them much myself. When was I last angry or sad? Now let me just think ...

THE MANIPULATOR

The only way that I can get attention from people is by sulking and crying and making lots of fuss. When I was a child I felt as though I could never get enough love, because I have such a big hole in me. Sometimes I would get attention by doing things like refusing to eat my dinner or put on my clothes.

Later in life: I really don't know what I want apart from needing you to notice me. I think I am happiest when I am trying to get your attention. And I will always try to get it, by fair means or by foul.

THE DREAMER

I spend a lot of my time day-dreaming. I feel comfortable doing that because I find life down here harsh and a bit difficult. I can easily get lost in my own little world.

Later in life: I often forget to keep appointments and lose my keys. People say I'm absent-minded— what was that you were saying? Sorry... my mind was somewhere else .

THE HURT CHILD

I am almost certain to be in you somewhere. Nobody really listened to me because they were too busy, or didn't understand, or were too tired, and I felt rejected. Now I've built a wall around myself, because I feel safer behind that wall.

Later in life: I sometimes feel depressed and isolated. It's difficult to let people in, so I can be sarcastic or a bit rude and difficult. I often make light of what I am really feeling, so people don't know. Yes, I would like to feel safe and free.

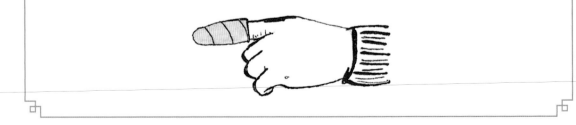

Finding your inner child

Reconnection to your Inner Child is not asking you to become childish again but to regain some of the child-like qualities that were squashed down, blocked off, buried and never allowed free expression. Those buried feelings stand between us and our expansion into soulfulness. Meeting up with your inner Divine Child—and it may turn out to be a tribe of children, all of different ages—it is as if some part of you that has been absent returns home. We are our own best parents now. We, as adults, are the best people to understand the needs of those parts of us that got left behind and frozen in the past.

Meeting up with your own inner Child or Children is like finding the missing pieces of a jigsaw and there is a powerful sense of being 'more' somehow, as one by one they feel safe enough to become part of your life again. If you have photographs of yourself at whatever age your Inner Child appears to be, dig them out and put them somewhere where you can remind yourself, frequently, of his or her presence. Talking to him or her as if they were around (talk to them silently, in your mind, if there are others nearby who might think you have gone mad) and include them in your daily life somehow is all part of the reintegration of the energy that became frozen and static all those years ago. This re-collection of 'parts' of ourselves is sometimes referred to as soul retrieval work.

What did your child enjoy doing? Can you remember? Allow yourself (and her or him) to do those things again. So who thinks that's silly? Your stuffy grown-up inner critic and judge who is probably mimicking one of your parents?

Inner Child work in therapy has proved to be an extremely potent and dynamic way of releasing patterns from the past.

Soul focus:
The innocence and vulnerability of our Inner Child leads us back to soul.

The next guided journey to record for yourself takes you to find an inner sanctuary. It will be a place of peace, tranquillity, love and safety, a special place that you can return to at any time to recollect those qualities. It is an appropriate meeting place for your Inner Child to re-establish contact with you. He or she may wish to stay in this place when you come back into everyday consciousness, or they may like to hold your hand and come with you. When you next find yourself in a situation that might have threatened or frightened that little person into 'splitting off' or hiding deep within, just imagine that you are holding their hand—it will be different now you are there to reassure.

Prepare yourself as before (see Chapter 3, page 60) for this guided meditation.

Journey to the sanctuary to meet my inner child

✳ I take some deep easy breaths, allowing my body to relax, and gently close my eyes. I take another deeper breath, to relax my mind. My breathing takes me to a deep, quiet place inside.

✳ I find myself on a path, a path that might be near the sea, by a river, or somewhere in the countryside. I am aware of the surface of the path underneath my feet. I can feel the warm sun and a gentle breeze on my face. I am aware of the sounds and smells of the earth; it's quiet and peaceful. I am on my way to a very special place, which I may find in an open space, in a glade or in a hollow. It has a special energy. When I arrive at this place, I feel relaxed and peaceful. I then become aware of the presence of a small child. I wonder how this small person will approach me, how does she (or he) look? I let her come towards me, how does she feel about this meeting? I let her say what she might want to say, either in words or some other way. Perhaps she has been waiting for some time for this meeting with me. I will spend some time with her now, allowing myself to be open to whatever this little person may need from me at this moment. (give yourself some space on the tape for this meeting and conversation). When she has told me what she needs from me, I will ask her if she would like to come back into the outside world with me, or whether she would like to meet me again in this safe sanctuary. If this little person of mine would rather stay here in this place, I will promise to come and see her again, or perhaps she would like to take my hand and walk back along the path with me, knowing that it is safe now, she has the love that she needs and that I will look after her.

Meditating on our inner child, or children helps us access our deeper needs as adults.

✴ Now I find myself becoming aware of my body, I feel centered and balanced. I feel as if I have connected with a part of myself that has been away for a while. I now start to feel my body on the chair and my feet on the ground. I hear the sounds of everyday life again. When I feel ready, I will open my eyes.

NOTE

Take some quiet time and go back in your mind to the point at which you were born. Then move forward allowing the subconscious right brain to float up images of land-mark situations. Start with the first seven-year period and see what you can remember about your childhood. How did you get love and attention if it wasn't freely available? Do you still look for love in this way?

When you have reclaimed one of your "lost" inner children make sure that they know they are home by making yourself aware of their presence until you feel they have become part of you again. Stop to watch a squirrel, feed the birds and observe children playing. It's not being silly to be childlike now and again.

CHAPTER 8

Karma and Reincarnation

What is karma and reincarnation?

Karma is the bank account of the soul that you bring down to earth in order to find balance. Reincarnation is the journey of a soul from one form, or body, to another.

What are the benefits?

Knowing that you were Queen Nefertiti in a previous life is not necessarily helpful. The point of understanding karma and reincarnation is to have a precious awareness of the lessons we may need to learn in this life. It can help you identify your place in a wider and older universe.

Do soul mates exist?

Yes: these are people you are destined to meet in order for you to grow as people. Soul mates are not alike—they can be very different people who can learn much from one another.

The earliest record of reincarnation comes from the ancient Egyptians, Hindus, Buddhists, Chinese Taoists, Jews, Greeks, Romans, Aboriginals, Native American Indians, Theosophists, Sufis, Zoroastrians, Rosicrucians, Freemasons and many, many more who have a history of belief in reincarnation, karma and the evolution of the soul. Past civilizations accepted re-birth as naturally as they accepted the ebb and flow of the sea, the daily appearance of the sun and moon, and the cycles of the year.

The "soul exchanges one man for another man, so that the life of humanity is continued always by means of the same soul" was written by St Gregory of Nazaianus in the 4th century. However by AD553, the Second Christian Council of Constantinople, presided over by Emperor Justinian, declared that all beliefs in immortality were heresies. He believed that citizens who would have another chance to live might be less obedient and law-abiding than those who believed in a single Judgement Day for all.

Almost all the passages in the Bible that made reference to reincarnation were edited out at this point. If you think you have only got one shot at this event called Life, you are more likely to pay attention to those who are in control of telling you how to live it. If you wanted to contact God in those days, you had to do it through the intercession of directory enquiries—the priests and clergy. This approach brought about several centuries of persecution in the "Holy War" of the Inquisition. The insistence of Christian religion that we are born into sin, and that salvation could only be acquired through confession and penance, that a certain number of sins committed in a lifetime meant either eternal damnation or years spent in the fires of purgatory, is quite an extraordinary departure from the love, compassion, and peace taught by its originator.

A bird is flight is a common symbol of the departure of the soul from the earthly body.

The mysteries of life and rebirth

Great minds have pondered on the mysteries of birth, life and rebirth since the beginning of recorded history, and probably before that. Great philosophers such as Pythagoras, Socrates and Plato through to D.H. Lawrence, Bertrand Russell and Carl Jung freely accepted the belief of "I am here now, and have been here before."

Today's research suggests that two-thirds of the world's population believe in past, present and future lives. Gradually, psychologists, doctors, psychiatrists and therapists have documented their clinical evidence and brought what was previously considered forbidden, irrational, or just plain fantasy, into the mainstream of current thinking. Past life regression therapy no longer belongs in the compartment labelled "New Age Flaky Mysticism."

One such psychologist, Dr Roger Woolger, who is an Oxford University graduate and Jungian analyst, says that he has had a positive response to a "remarkable range of human problems" using past life regression in his psychotherapy practice. He also states that it is not necessary to believe in reincarnation for regression therapy to be effective. All that is required is a belief in the healing power of the unconscious mind through which memories are accessed. Simply following the experiences that present themselves to the client "as if they were a dream" is enough. What is important is getting in touch with those blocks, or complexes of energy, that are preventing us from living life to the full. Telling the rational mind that "this is only a dream" allows it to let go of its control and gives the psyche or soul the opportunity to bring old wounds carried forward from the past into conscious awareness. Once in conscious awareness, they can be released.

The starting points for accessing these old memories we may be holding are thought to be found in either body symptoms, and repetitive, irrational thoughts or negative feelings that appear to have no foundation.

Marks from past lives

Strange lumps, bumps, scars, and birthmarks often bear witness to how a past-life personality died—especially in the case of a violent death. Dr Stevenson, probably one of the best-known researchers into reincarnation, has investigated hundreds of cases, most of which concern children. We know that the child still remembers Home. Dr Stevenson began his research interviews with children by asking them, "How was it when you were big?". From this starting point, information about people, places, events, and even knowledge of a language that had never been heard by the child would come forth.

He reports on a child, born into this life with a scar round his neck, who claimed to have had his throat cut in a previous existence. Another child described an attack where a knife was thrust into his chest and dragged downward towards his stomach. He too was born with a jagged scar exactly like the wound of his description. There is a wealth of literature now available on the whole subject of past lives for those who are interested.

At the point of death of the physical body, the soul leaves, carrying any imprints of trauma it has experienced in that lifetime. These are the sort of thoughts that stamp themselves onto the soul when they are experienced with intense feelings: "I must hide," "I'm responsible for this," "They all hate me," "I'm going to drown," "I can't get out," "He's going to leave me." Dying with a powerful thought such as, "She has betrayed me" as you are stabbed to death by your lover, may be carried forward into another lifetime as an unreasonable fear of trusting another in a relationship. Perhaps if you have died in poverty and starvation in a previous existence you are carrying the seemingly unreasonable thought: "I haven't got enough money. I will die if I don't get some more."

There may be intense feelings still held in the body—the stab in the back, the sense of being choked or suffocated, or tension in the

Believing in reincarnation means we take with us soul issues and some physical characteristics from previous lives.

pelvic area as a result of a sexual assault. This may appear in the current lifetime as restricted breathing, odd stabbing pains, or a fear about sexuality. Or there may be feelings of rage, grief, betrayal or loss that leave with the soul and reappear in subsequent lifetimes as inexplicable echoes of previous experience.

Your feelings about people and places offer clues to past life experiences that might have been tremendous or terrifying. Always feeling threatened by those in authority may reflect an overbearing parent, but that may not be the root cause of these feelings. Perhaps you were

Common phobias - of water, spiders, heights— can be attributed to issues or experiences from a previous existence.

done to death by some lord or master in the past. Or maybe there are places that you have visited that have a "familiar" feel although you have never been there before, or you may have come across someone and you "know" that you have met them before.

Past-life therapy

Using past life experiences as a tool in therapy has become almost mainstream practice in the US. It is different from the type of regression that simply satisfies your curiosity about who you might have been. So what if you were King Arthur or Queen Nefertiti, interesting people to be, but so what? Past life therapy is a powerful way of getting to the cause of symptoms that you may not have been able to access through more conventional methods. If regular introspection into present life circumstances has failed to bring change, perhaps deeper exploration will help. We have a violent history and it is unlikely that the soul has come through those dark ages of war, torture, deprivation and pestilence without carrying some unfinished business forward. Our current life conditions, the parents and environment we chose at a soul level, will encourage us to address the issues of forgiveness, compassion and release of fear and grief. It is important to remember that we are not victims, we volunteered for this!

Why consult a past-life therapist?

People consult past life therapists for many different reasons. Delving into past lives during therapy can positively affect all aspects of life. It may be your health, understanding relationships, releasing creativity, or overcoming your fear of death. By reliving a powerful or talented past life, you may release those inherent qualities within for use today, and involving the body in this process also helps to amplify the effect. How differently your body will feel now, standing in front of that crowd knowing you are loved and respected, compared with the past-life experience of being showered with eggs and tomatoes, or even stones—those belonged to the life story, the soul drama, that built up the complex you felt around public speaking. The problem that you are hoping to solve may have been carried through several lifetimes, and may take more than one session to clear.

Sometimes it is not appropriate to know at a conscious level why we are locked into a relationship that is driving us mad. Perhaps this is an opportunity to become more in touch with your soul for understanding and guidance.

Some past life therapists use hypnosis, and others do not. At all times the "observer self" should be in control and able to pull you back to your physical reality. Some therapists use the technique of asking their clients to re-run the murder, rape, or abandonment scene that they have connected with, creating an action replay of how they would now like to remember the scene. This may clear the painful complex from the memory bank and work for well for some people. For others, "living" through that experience, allowing the body to feel the pain again, letting the emotions really feel the betrayal or grief that was experienced back in time, and then moving to the other side of death of the physical body may have a profoundly cathartic effect. This can help you to understand at last why, for example, you have always had this fear of rats, or why, you can't get on with your father.

Perhaps the most significant part of past life regression work is the experience of going to the "interlife state." It is, of course, going Home.

Recovery of these experiences brings about a change in consciousness and an attitude of compassion because here, beyond the confines of the physical body, everything takes on a different perspective. In the Tibetan Buddhist tradition this interlife place is known as the Bardo. Drawn from the physical plane by a clear light, it is here that the soul can meet with others from its group, and come to understand the difficult and painful issues that might have plagued it when it was in its body. For many people this transforms their view of death and the mistaken notion that there is some kind of a panel of judges who will apportion retribution.

However, the only judge of our earthly behavior is our Self. The interlife experience is one of unconditional Love without judgment. Just as past life recall has become an available option for increasing numbers of people over the past few years, more and more people will undoubtedly be able to access interlife consciousness in the near future. The changes that this experience will bring about are something to look forward to.

In Tibetan Buddhism, the interlife state is known as the Bardo, a place where you review your experiences on earth. Here, the soul meets with other souls.

The law of karma

Intrinsic to the understanding of reincarnation is the understanding of the Law of Karma. "Whatsoever a man soweth, that shall he also reap," said St Paul in his Epistle to the Galatians. The Law of Karma is a divine system of balance, counter-balance and perfect justice; a system in which nothing happens by accident. It is cause and effect simultaneously, because every action we take generates a force of energy that returns to us in kind, in the same way as a boomerang. It is the law used to justify inequalities. It is not a law of punishment for past life crimes. It is the law by which the soul may ex-perience both ends of a polarity, both ends of a pendulum swing, both sides of a coin. If you have been a tyrant and an abuser of power in the past, you (the soul) need to know what it is like to be on the receiving end of tyranny and misuse of power. But it is not God who decides that you will be punished for past misdeeds. It is the soul itself that requires the mirror of life to reflect back what adjustments need to be made. It is not a judge in the sky that monitors our deeds and actions, it is we ourselves who have an inner scale of justice that monitors our integrity. It is we who are always trying to balance the scales within us.

Understanding this Law takes us beyond judgement of others. How do we know what anyone else's soul is bringing forward for attention? Behind every abuser is the one who has been abused. When you look at the case histories of current child abusers it generally reveals a background of a damaged or "different" childhood. This is not to say that these acts should be condoned, but it

helps to bring in a wider, deeper perspective. Karma provides us with a kaleidoscope of opportunities to experience incarnation in a physical body. Over and over again, we play hero, villain, queen and slave, and everything in between. This gradually hones our personalities. We always have the free will and choice to shed those clothes that don't fit any more, the negative bits and pieces of ourselves that tip the scales into imbalance and that keep the pendulum swinging. We never take on in any one lifetime more than we can cope with. Dr Elisabeth Kubler-Ross, author of *Living with Death & Dying*, says "If you experience losses, you can take the pain and learn to accept it, not as a curse or punishment, but as a gift to you, a gift with a very specific purpose."

It may not feel like a gift of course, but any event or relationship that carries a "charge" is sure to be a karmic re-run. Let's say the soul recorded her experience of a lifetime on a floppy disc. After removing the disc at death of the physical body, there is unfinished business concerning certain responses or events in that particular lifetime. To correct the balance, that disc has to be brought up on the screen again so that the saved information may be changed. You are not going to get a re-run of being burned at the stake as a witch, but tied into that traumatic event are powerful feelings perhaps about forgiveness, fear of being true to your nature, betrayal, and so on. So the soul will draw towards it a situation which echoes that past event in order that it can be re-recorded, or edited if you like. This time someone has (out of jealousy) exposed you at work for not toeing the line. Will you be fired (a rather different type of firing) without saying

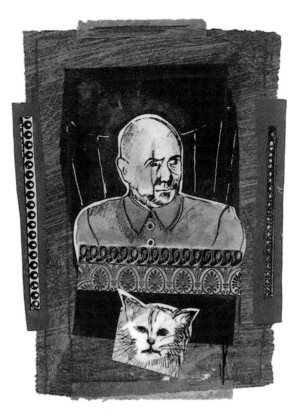

Who are the bad guys? There can be a common theme of tyrants or oppressors that the soul re-experiences.

anything, or do you confront your betrayer—how will you handle it this time? In this way, you get a re-run of a situation in order to experience a more positive response.

Memories of the past

It seems that the memories of past experience are close to the surface now. Perhaps 100 monkeys have accessed their karmic history and feel freer as a result! It is said that the vibrational energies coming into the planet, and therefore our own energy bodies, have changed in frequency so that we can prepare for the next step in the evolution of consciousness. We are being asked to "re-member" who we really are. It is as if each

of us has been living our lives at the end of a long octopus tentacle. We have become so absorbed in the sand, the shells and the other creatures that live at this level that we have forgotten that we are also part of the octopus.

Young or old souls?

We sometimes make reference to people as being "old souls" or "young souls." When our souls first take on a physical form, perhaps we are not given much choice as to specific circumstances, conditions and personality traits. The soul has chosen to experience life on Earth, contained within a dense material body, governed by the laws and principles of the planet and seemingly with a factory-installed implant stating "thou shalt not remember who you are." "Thou shall also experience time in a linear way and you have got about three-score years and ten to see how you get on. Now sign on the dotted line!" If we knew (intellectually) that we were here for the purpose of growing spiritually, if we were able to remember where we came from, we would not experience our lives in the way that we do. It is only by living on this physical plane that the soul grows in knowledge and stature.

Gradually, lifetime by lifetime, the soul builds up this bank of experience. After the death of the physical body, the soul draws up its balance sheet of life in that particular body. It will subtract what it has already dealt with and carry forward what is unfinished business in its journey of growing and becoming. Life on Earth has been about measuring experience, one against another. How can we know about separation if we have never experienced unity? Joy is measured against pain and freedom against imprisonment. Knowing only love, how would we ever understand someone who felt unloved and desperate? It is here on Earth that we learn to value the positive through experiencing the negative. If you have starved in this or another lifetime, you will value food and not waste it.

Through lifetimes, every facet of human event and emotion is included—doubt, fear, hate, rejection, loss, despair, jealousy, and punishment, as well as love, joy, power, success, tranquility, and peace. It was the American prophet Edgar Cayce (known as the Sleeping Prophet) who responded to the question "From which side of my family do I inherit most?" with the following: "You have inherited most from yourself, not from your family. The family is only a river through which the soul flows."

Why do people get chronically ill?

This is a difficult one as no would choose to get chronically ill, just for the experience. Let us take cancer, for example. The soul has clothed itself in this lifetime with a personality that chooses to repress certain emotions. These repressed emotions build up as clots of energy or static in the subtle bodies and may eventually manifest themselves as cancer. Of course there have been choices all along the way up to this point, but now comes the major challenge: having the courage to face the fear and overcome it. Dr Simonton has done some amazing research using visualization techniques, and reports the most remarkable outcome from patients who have beaten cancer in this way. He says that they undergo a kind of transformation. Overcoming huge obstacles produces a sense of inner strength, which is the soul feeling fortified. The fear of death from disease has been overcome. This feeling at death, of being victimised by fate, the body or life in general has been turned into a strength.

Jungian psychotherapist Roger Woolger refers to these past life experiences as unfinished "soul dramas." In past life soul dramas we may come across the same character in different guises. This is the wagon train effect, because we work in soul groups. Those we are in contact with have been with us before. The relationship we have to these other souls gives us the chance to work through unfinished business.

What about soul mates?

The whole nature of relationships is changing, as women look for equal partnership instead of being content to accept supporting roles. This doesn't make it easy for either men or women. Couples used to refer to one another as "my better half," implying that they are only half a person without the other. At the level of the soul, our other half is sometimes known as a twin flame. Soozi Holbeche in Journeys Through Time says that twin souls rarely incarnate together unless they are either at the end of a particular cycle of evolution, or have a specific—usually spiritual—task to accomplish. Twin souls are in such harmony that if they lived life on Earth together they would do little besides look longingly into one another's eyes. They would literally think and be as one. Not much would be accomplished and there would be no desire to get out into the world. Soul mates are sometimes mistaken for twin souls and meeting with a soul mate

Soul mates are those who have an immediate knowledge of one another—a person whom, on a soul level, they have met before.

always means growth. It can sometimes be extremely uncomfortable growth, however as soul mates often have instant recognition of one another—it is someone we have known for many lifetimes, after all. The closest and dearest of our friends are the ones who have the courage and love to point out our weaknesses and encourage our strengths. A soul mate will be your mirror—he or she will reflect back to you those areas of yourself that need attention. It is as if there is an enormously strong invisible connection between you that makes it impossible to walk away. You have to look at the issues that are being brought up between you. By honestly communicating your thoughts and feelings to one another the relationship may grow into a permanent partnership, or alternatively you may recognize the value of your coming together, knowing that there is other work to be done on separate journeys.

You may also encounter one member in your current family whose personality and actions drive you to distraction. It is possible that this soul has incarnated (out of love) to play the "bad guy" in your life so that you have the opportunity to come to terms with another aspect of love—compassion and forgiveness. The sooner we stop judging everyone from an earthly physical perspective, and remember that behind every mask is another soul, experiencing the same world of separation from Home as we are, the sooner we can live our lives openly and freely instead of from behind fortress walls and defended boundaries. We are all part of the same Universe in the same way that a heart cell is part of the same body as a toenail cell—one is by no means better than another.

Soul focus:
The soul gains experience through many lifetimes on Earth.

The next visualization tape to make for yourself will guide you through to a positive past life experience. Remember that you are in control of the experience at all times and you can simply open your eyes to bring you back into everyday consciousness. If you find your left brain kicking in and telling you this is "just your imagination," politely tell it you are going through with this experience, "as if it were a dream." Listen to the tape several times—you may need to go over a specific lifetime more than once, or you may like to access more than one lifetime. If you want to spend more time in the interlife state, push the pause button on your tape machine—you won't lose the connection—and restart it when you are ready to come back to this reality. It is important, at the end of this visualization, to ask yourself what relevance it has to your current life, and what might that past life character have to say to you in your contemporary casing. Write down what happens to you in your journal. Make yourself comfortable in a chair (see Chapter three, page 42) to start the visualization.

Journey into my archives

✳ I make myself comfortable. When I am ready, I gently close my eyes.

✳ I take some deep easy breaths and let any tension drain out of me into the floor. As my body starts to relax and I begin to feel calmer, I can start to remember. I invite my unconscious mind to bring forward a past life experience from my memory bank, an experience that it is useful for me to recollect, one that will bring understanding and insight perhaps—a positive experience. If I feel uncomfortable at any time, I will simply open my eyes and return to my normal

Meditating on a past life can help us discover who we are and who we have been.

waking state. I am completely in control. As I breathe slowly and deeply, I imagine that I am breathing my life force up through my toes and into my feet, then into my ankles, and my knees. I continue breathing up the life force through my thighs, into my pelvis and buttocks, then up through my abdomen to my waist. I bring it up through my arms to my shoulders, letting my shoulders remember how it feels to be free. Now I take my consciousness to my throat and neck. My lower body starts to feel as if it has dissolved, now I breathe into my jaw, my cheeks, my eyeballs, right through to the back of my head. I let it rest there for a moment like a ball, a bubble of consciousness, just floating, drifting easily, gently, filled with peace, like a balloon, lifting higher and higher, drifting through time and space.

✳ I am free of the limitations of time-bound reality, I am in that place where the past, the present and the future co-exist. I find myself in a place with many doorways, doorways that are gateways into different life experiences from the past or the future. I notice which of these doorways seems to draw me towards it and stop in front of this doorway, feeling relaxed and at peace, knowing I am in control of my experience. My mind is longer limited by time and space, and I can remember everything that happened to me. When I open the door and pass through it, I will enter another time frame, allowing my unconscious mind to choose the time, whether from this life or any other. I may go back to a time when a symptom of mine, a feeling or a troubling relationship first arose, or I may be going to recollect a time and place where I experienced joy, love, healing—wholeness. A place where there is no judgment. Going through the doorway now, I emerge into a light. I look down at my feet and notice what I am wearing on them, or are they bare? What sort of feet are they? What sort of legs are they attached to? I just let the image come together, moving up my body. I know whether this is the body of a man or a woman, I know what I'm wearing. I feel the quality of whatever it is that I am wearing, is it coarse or fine? I look at my hands, what sort of work do they do? Are they young or old? Now I look around myself, am I alone? Or is there someone else here with me? Where do I live? I can go backwards or forwards in time now, exploring any significant events. Who were the other people involved in this soul drama of mine? Do I recognize them? I build up the energy around the story as if I were dreaming a dream. (Give yourself some silent time on the tape for this exploration.)

✳ I go now to the end of that lifetime and experience my death. My soul leaves my body, and floats above it. I review that life, my thoughts and feelings, and I ponder on what lessons I was to learn. Do I need to forgive myself or anybody else for anything? I begin to feel the magnetism of a light above me, I am drawn towards it. It is the light of Home—wonderful, illuminated, joy and love without condition. I feel myself fill up with Light. (Give yourself some space on the tape to appreciate this experience).

✳ Soon it will be time for me to return to my body and the life that I am living at the moment. I become aware of my body sitting on the chair, my feet on the ground, and the sounds of external reality. When I open my eyes once again, I will be wide awake, alert and refreshed. I will be in full control of all my physical and psychological functions and I will remember everything that has happened.

NOTE

Look at difficult situations for their potential learning. Who do you have powerful connections with (comfortable and uncomfortable)? What experience does this bring you? Do you find that there is a consistent repeating pattern in your life regarding health, security or relationship? What places or cultures are you inexplicably drawn to? In difficult situations, can you get out of blaming, and try to see the wider picture?

Helpful practices

*A tree as big around as you
can reach starts with a small
seed; a thousand-mile journey
starts with one small step.*
Lao-tsu

This may be the last chapter of the book, but please don't stop when you have finished reading it. It is important to remember that the map is not the territory. Your individual experience is what is important to you and your soul, so use your judgment about what is appropriate for you. Remember, when you find a truth, there is that sense of "Aha! Yes!" If you only get a feeling of "So what?", then leave it alone. It is the "Aha's!" that are really important.

Perhaps as you have read this book you may have felt encouraged to explore, understand, and experience more; this is what spiritual growth is all about. It is expanding beyond who we think we are and becoming more of who we can be. This does not happen by dimming your light, or hiding it under a bushel. It means that your spiritual nature, your soul, needs to become part of your daily experience.

According to the great cosmic calendar of the ancient Mayan civilization, we are now in the last baktun (144,000 day period) of our epoch. They named this time the "Transformation of Matter." We can transform our "matters" by introducing our soul, and then we will see more clearly what it is that really matters.

Looking inside

In our hectic modern world, we rush about filling our heads with concerns about the future that are based on our experience of the past. To get off this frantic merry-go-round that spins faster and faster in a world where technology advances at a mind-boggling speed, we need a little discipline—a word that has uncomfortable connotations. Start with taking just a few minutes each day, if that is all you can manage, but approach it with due reverence.

Perhaps it would be helpful to go over the reminders that come at the end of each chapter to help you with your practice—because a practice it has to become. We are creatures of habit and we tend to get better at things we do regularly. Here are some suggestions.

MAKING A SACRED SPACE: If you haven't done this already, make a special place, a special chair or pillow that you sit in or on for your daily reflection time. It can be as simple or elaborate as you like. Light a candle as a symbolic gesture that you are about to enter your own inner sacred space. Here you might like to listen to some appropriate music, a guided meditation tape, or simply sit in the silence of your own contemplation. Make sure you will not be interrupted and pay attention to your posture and breathing as outlined in Chapters 1 and 2. This will help prevent you from falling asleep. Your body needs to be relaxed, but your mind needs to be aware and alert. Going through a ritual, however short, gives a message to your soul or psyche that you are preparing to move from one state of consciousness to another.

Creating a sacred space for meditation is a physical manifestation of your desire to connect with your soul. Your space can be as simple as a favorite chair.

DAILY PRACTICE: Time spent meditating before you start your day means that you set off into your life out there with an awareness of the presence of soul inside. Time spent focusing your awareness before breakfast means that you will have a better chance of going through the day more mindfully. Being more mindful, even just until lunchtime, means that you can make conscious decisions, rather than reactions produced by the tapes of past experience. Making even a simple statement such as "Thy will be done" in your contemplation time aligns with higher perspective beyond the density of three-dimensional reality. "I have everything

I need" takes the edge off the frantic skirmish for more of everything;. "Be still and know that I am God" changes perspective in a profound way.

The end of the day is the other important soul time. Sitting quietly, in stillness, you can quieten your busy mind and review your day. What was good about it? What might you have done differently? This time is not for beating yourself up with "should-have's" and "ought-to-have's." We get it wrong before we get it right and our inner critics and judges are not aspects of our soul. They belong to the ego and the past. People grow in confidence when they are encouraged, not when they are continually criticised. This practice at the end of the day also ensures that we don't go to sleep with a load of unfinished business disturbing or worrying us.

BEING AWARE: Perhaps this is the most important attribute of all to develop. By being aware, the invisible becomes visible and the unconscious becomes known. When we live with awareness, we expand our consciousness of who we are. Without awareness, we are the victims of the unconscious programmes that run our lives. What presses your buttons? Have you ever stopped to work out why that might be? We go on re-acting in the same old way every time something happens that presses that button. With awareness, at least you can choose if you want to do or say the same thing yet again. It also means we become

Seeing the Divine in simple things is important if we are to integrate soulfulness with everyday living. We can enjoy the energy of being fully in the present, rather than taking refuge in dreaminess.

more present in our lives. Often we will stand in the bedroom and ask "What have I come in here for?" and have to go back to where we started in order to remember! Becoming aware of the Divine in all things—even when you're washing up—creates a sense of connection to something wider and greater than ourselves. If you find yourself getting caught up in the maelstrom of life, just stop for a moment and repeat to yourself: "I breathe in peace ... I breathe out love." Doing this will help to bring you into your center of focus. It will take you out of your head and into your body, calming, balancing, and making you "aware."

BALANCE: This is another useful thing to be aware of. We live in a world of duality: black and white, right and wrong, happy and sad, pendulum swings, always measuring one state against another. If we do not do something perfectly, then we have failed (says the ego, speaking from the solar plexus). We put our feelings into boxes labelled "good" and "bad."

Feelings are feelings, and what is important is that we allow ourselves to feel them, and express them appropriately. Have a look, also, at the balance between life as a human being and a human doing. By continually searching for balance in our lives, by saying, "On the one hand I have this, and on the other I have that" we move into the perspective of the see-saw—standing in the middle, we find balance. Instead of dividing life into positive and negative, we remember that both are needed in equal amounts.

There is also a point of balance that needs to be found between the twin travelers that live in our heads—the left and right hemispheres of the brain. We need our left-brain to deal with daily issues that require the more masculine qualities of logic, analysis, and attention to detail, but it is also vital to consider the intuitive, visionary, imaginative lady who lives in the right mind.

ACCEPTANCE: This is another key word, and it is about acceptance of ourselves as we are, first of all, and acceptance of others as they are. We cannot change anyone but ourselves, and it is none of our business to even attempt it. We have no idea what is in another person's karmic script. If they are here to work through the issue of overcoming the need to control or bully others, then providing them with a victim will not help them come home to themselves.

Acceptance does not mean complacence. It means saying, "This is the way things are— I will take action (or do nothing) in accordance with the directions from my soul." Honest communication always brings positive results. It's not what you say, but the way that you say

it. And don't forget—the work of the soul is all about remembering.

DREAMS: Paying attention to your dreams is important. Some dreaming is simply the unconscious mind clearing the accumulated waste of our daily thoughts. Then there are what Carl Jung calls "big dreams." These are significant messages coming from the unconscious mind to give our earthly personality important information. The difficulty is in the interpretation, and since dreams do not appear with a dictionary of meaning, we have to do the best we can. Only you can fully interpret the meaning of your own dreams. Reading a book on dream symbols will give you an idea of what the symbols means generally, but you need to look for the "Aha!" experience that means you have stepped on a Truth (for you) and made a connection that brings information from the depths of the psyche to the light of conscious thought.

The language of the dream, rather like the body, is metaphor and symbol—because it speaks through the right brain. If there are characters in the dream that you recognize, they are there as a representative of an aspect of your self. Your mother appearing in a dream may have nothing to do with your actual mother, but speaks about the mothering part of you, or whatever your feelings about your mother are. A telephone in your dream may not mean you must phone someone. More likely it is saying something about communication between aspects of your self and the outside world.

Since dreams have a tendency to vaporize as we start to wake up, write them down as soon as you open your eyes, and if possible make a drawing or two. Keeping a dream notebook by your bed means you can catch and record them. As you write the dream down, relive it in your mind. Go back into it to get as much of the story as possible, and notice your feelings.

Healthy mind, body, and soul

Becoming aware of the health of these three aspects of ourselves means they can work as a team. They all need rest, exercise and nourishment and a sense of communion. This is the meaning of wholistic (holistic) healthcare.

THE MIND: From time immemorial our masterful minds have held sway in a world where accumulation and analysis of facts and figures get the credit. It was Einstein of all people who said "I want to know the mind of God. The rest is detail." The fact that he also valued the importance of imagination over knowledge demonstrates his understanding of the power of the right hemisphere of the brain—the cradle of inspiration. That inspiration manifests through the action of the left brain— there has to be a marriage of our minds, the left and right, positive and negative coming together to create. Scientific breakthroughs, artistic masterpieces, even creative stir-fries are the products of left and right working together. Our minds need rest as well as stimulation. Give your mind a break, don't drive it into breakdown. What does it enjoy doing? If you find your head is taking over your life, get back into your body by breathing in and breathing out ... not only will you be able to think more clearly using conscious breathing, you will also give your brain more oxygen to do so.

Constant, random thoughts can interfere with our connection with a peaceful sense of self. Many of our thoughts are repetitive, but we can make a conscious decision to think differently.

Remember that the body metabolizes your thoughts. All those 30,000 thoughts—does such a large percentage of them have to be the same as yesterday? Rather a waste of thinking time, wouldn't you say?

THE BODY: This mostly needs acknowledgement and awareness. Becoming conscious of how your body speaks to you will mean that you not only have a healthier home for your soul, but also that you can become aware of the toxic thoughts and feelings that are scrambling the air waves of the subtle anatomy, preventing intake of the pranic (energetic) life force. Becoming more aware of sensations, means you experience more, consciously. Touch the silky petal of that flower; notice the feeling of water on your face. Does your hair like being brushed? Does your body feel like digesting a cream bun or brown rice today? Is it tired? Is it cramped? Have your feet had enough of being confined to their shoe-shaped prisons?

There are a hundred other questions you can ask that will take you out of your mind and into your senses. Our bodies are both our vehicle for experiencing life as a soul on Earth and for also expressing who we are. We can't do much without them. Don't be condescending about your body's needs. You live in a beautifully orchestrated, highly complex miracle of organized energy that was personally designed for your purpose in this short dream we call Life. Listen to it, look after it and above all, let it breathe.

THE SOUL: This part of us needs to experience a sense of sacredness in every day, ordinary things—taking part with heart and soul. Being aware of our soul draws us into the axis of our wheel. From here we can see the value in life's challenges and express ourselves as authentic individuals, instead of trying to conform. It's good to be eccentric, says the soul; it's all right to be different. Becoming aware of your soulfulness does not mean casting your eyes to heaven and divorcing yourself from reality. On the contrary, it means there is more juice in life. A deep sense of joy at being with real friends, having good discussions, fulfilling work or being alone are what delights the soul—in fact, any

experience that gives us a sense of connection. This sense of connection reminds us of "Home." When we have that sense of being at Home in ourselves, all our journeys, short or long, are exciting —and bring with them a sense of having traveled somewhere different. It's safe to travel anywhere when you know where Home is.

Remember to listen to your feelings. Allow them to be felt, rather than denying them or projecting them on to others. Listen to your highest thoughts, and become the observer of your experiences.

Becoming who you really are is a process. Nothing changes from this to that in the wink of an eye. Like a transforming caterpillar, we are experiencing the emergence (although it sometimes feels like an emergency) of a new way of being. We may have been asleep in the chrysalis for a while, unaware of the transformation taking place. Now it is time to wake up to the fact that there is a reality beyond the one to which we have become so attached. Becoming aware of this other reality, however, does not take us out of the world; on the contrary, we become a part of it, but in a different way. Having the courage to emerge from our chrysalis enables us to let go of our limited caterpillar vision, so that we can see and experience life from a wider perspective.

Step by step, we become more familiar with this new perspective, and as each of us decides to move outside the herd instinct and become something different, the herd, too, will change its ways.

Further Reading

CHAPTER 1
Hindu Yogi—Science of Breath Yogi Ramacharaka,
    L.N. Fowler & Co

CHAPTER 2
Your Body Speaks your Mind Debbie Shapiro,
    Piatkus
Quantum Healing, Deepak Chopra, Bantam Books
Heal Your Body, Louise Ha, Eden Grove Editions
The Power of the Mind to Heal Joan Boryensko,
    Axis Publishing
The Tibetan Book of Living and Dying Sogyal
    Rinpoche, Rider Books
Peace is Every Step Thich Nhat Hanh, Rider
Meditation in a Changing World William Bloom
    Gothic Image
Moon Over Water Jessica Macbeth, Gateway Books
Teach yourself to Meditate Eric Harrison, Piatkus

CHAPTER 3
Man's Subtle Bodies & Centres Ivanov, Prosveta
Principles of Vibrational Healing Clare G Harvey
    and Amanda Cochrane, (Thorsons)
The Art of Psychic Protection Judy Hall,
    Findhorn Press
Hands of Light Barbara Ann Brennan,
    Bantam Books

CHAPTER 4
The Elements of the Chakras Naomi Ozaniek
Frontiers of Health Dr Christine Page,
    C.W. Daniel Co
Working with your Chakras Ruth White, Piatkus

CHAPTER 5
Your Healing Power Jack Angel, Pitches
The Complete Healer David Furlong, Pitches
The Healing Power Within G R Bolton,
    Homer Publishing

CHAPTER 6
Mediumship Made Simple Ivy Northage, College
    of Psychic Studies
Channelling for Everyone Tony Neate, Piatkus
Develop Your Intuition & Psychic Powers
    David Furlong, Bloomsbury
The Art of Psychic Protection Judy Hall,
    Findhorn Press
Psychic Protection William Bloom, Piatkus
As I See It Betty Balcombe, Piatkus
Insight & Intuition Julie Soskin, Light Publishing

CHAPTER 7
Homecoming John Bradshaw, Piatkus
The Inner World of Childhood Frances Wickes,
    Coventure

CHAPTER 8
Other Lives, Other Selves Dr Roger Woolger,
    Aquarian Press
Principles of Past Life Therapy Judy Hall, Thorsons
Hands Across Time, The Soulmate Enigma Judy Hall,
    Findhorn Press
Through Time into Healing, Brian Weiss, Piatkus
Journeys Through Time Soozi Holbeche, Piatkus

CHAPTER 9
Vibrational Medicine Richard Gerber, Bear & Co)
Power of Gems & Crystals Soozi Holbeche, Piatkus
Healing with Crystals Liz Simpson, Gaia

Index

acceptance 156
astral body 54–55
auras 44–61, 64, 65, 97
  auric egg 52, 58–60
  bodies (levels) 48, 52–57
  colors 48
  depletion 49, 50
  energizers 51
  waterfall cleansing exercise 56, 123
automatic writing 104, 114, 115
awareness, living with 35, 39, 40, 64, 155

balance, state of 16, 94, 155–156
belief systems 55
body–mind link 8–27
  bodily renewal 11
  body language 13–14, 16, 17
  body-memory 21–23
  brain function 12–13, 21, 36, 37, 55, 113
  car metaphor 10, 14
  homeostasis 16
  inner child 22–23, 126–137
breathing 28–39
  baby breathing 30–31
  conscious breathing 32–33, 34–35
  emotional states and 31–32, 35
  meditation and 30, 36–39
  mind connection 32

chakras 62–91
  Base (Root) chakra 66–68, 86
  Brow (Third Eye) chakra 39, 82–83, 88, 108, 116
  chakra healing 62, 91
  Crown chakra 84–85, 88
  crystals and 91
  Heart chakra 75–78, 87, 97
  minor chakras 65
  Sacral chakra 69–71, 87
  Solar Plexus chakra 13, 72–74, 87
  Throat chakra 79–81, 88
channeling 108, 114, 118
chi see energy
clairaudience and clairvoyance 115, 116, 118
collective unconscious 46–47
crystals 90–91

dowsing 64, 111–112
dreams 55, 83, 116, 156–157

emotional sensitivity 112–113
emotional suppression 19, 23, 54
energy
  crystal energy 90
  energy-sensing exercise 53
  healing energy 92, 94, 95, 96, 108, 111
  personal energy fields see auras
  psychic energy 108, 110, 111–112
  universal energy field 46, 47, 106
  yin and yang 108
etheric body 52–53, 54

healing 92–103
  absent or distant healing 99
  chakra healing 62, 91
  hand-energizing exercise 98, 108
  healers 54, 92, 93, 95, 96
  healing energy 92, 94, 95, 96, 108, 111
  healing ritual 97–98
  painful areas 98
  with sound or color 99–101
  tuning in 94, 95, 102–103
healthy mind, body, and soul 14, 157–158

ill health 11, 14, 17–19, 66, 69, 72, 75, 79, 82, 84, 147
  see also healing
inner child 22–23, 126–137
  behavioural patterns 131–134
  reconnecting to 135, 136–137
intuition 116

karma and reincarnation 128, 138–153
  regression therapy 140, 143–144

love 22, 70, 76, 77, 78, 87, 130
  loving your enemy 123

meditations and visualizations 7, 33, 36–43, 56, 58–61, 83
  auric egg 58–60
  body–mind journey 24–27

breathing and 30, 36–39
centering prayer 40
daily practice 43, 154–155
healing tune-up 102–103
holy moment meditation 40
inner seeing exercise 116
intrusive thoughts 37, 38
journeying through the chakras 86–89
making a sacred space 43, 154
meeting your inner child 136–137
music and dancing meditation 42
past life experience 150–152
psychic bubble 121
through the psychic gateway 124–125
walking meditation 42
mental body 55
see also body–mind link

psychic abilities 107–108, 123
psychic internet 104–125
  channeling 108, 114, 118
  clairaudience and clairvoyance 115, 116, 118
  emotional sensitivity 112–113
  inner hearing 113–114
  problematic messages 114–115
  psychic energy 108, 110, 111–112
  psychic protection 120–123
  spirit guides 119–120
psychoneuroimmunology (PNI) 11

regression therapy 140, 143–144
relationships 70–71, 80, 87, 148–149
rhythm of life 47

sixth sense see psychic internet
soul body 57
soul mates 138, 148–149
spirit guides 119–120
spiritual growth 9, 153

yin and yang 21, 108